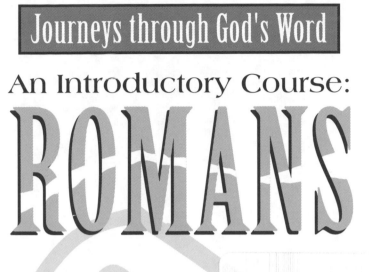

Journeys through God's Word

An Introductory Course:
ROMANS

D0796619

John
Scharlemann

CPH
SAINT LOUIS

Edited by Thomas J. Doyle

This publication is available in braille and in large print for the visually impaired. Write to the Library for the Blind, 1333 S. Kirkwood Rd., St. Louis, MO 63122-7295; or call 1-800-433-3954.

Copyright © 1999 Concordia Publishing House
3558 South Jefferson Avenue, St. Louis, MO 63118-3968
Manufactured in the United States of America

1   2   3   4   5   6   7   8   9   10   08   07   06   05   04   03   02   01   00   99

Contents

Introduction

The study of the Bible is nothing less than an exploration into the thoughts and desires of God for ordinary people like you and me. It takes us from this hardened and selfish world into the promise of a world where God's peace, justice, and mercy will be complete.

Delving into the Bible for the first time can be somewhat intimidating. We are taken to a distant past that is full of unfamiliar customs and traditions. We must become acquainted with a nation that viewed the world differently than many people do today. And we must begin to alter some of our current definitions to grasp the full meaning of our Lord's love and compassion.

As foreign as many customs and traditions might seem to us today, we will discover that people's natures remain the same. We are trapped today—as people were centuries ago—in an imperfect world where evil and pain seem all too prevalent. We, too, can view the world as meaningless and without hope. But Jesus Christ came to rescue the world from its quagmire, and His deliverance continues to change our lives. Pray that the Word of God will begin to alter your perspective. May His promises give you rich and lasting hope and joy!

How to Use This Study

The Study Guide will direct your study of Romans. The typical session is divided into five parts:

1. Approaching This Study
2. An Overview
3. Working with the Text
4. Applying the Message
5. Taking the Message Home

"Approaching This Study" is intended to whet the reader's appetite for the topics at hand. It leads participants into the world of the New Testament while summarizing the issues to be examined. "An Overview" summarizes the textual material used in each session. Before the text is examined in detail, it is viewed as a whole, allowing participants to "see the forest" before "exploring the trees." "Working with the Text" draws participants into deeper biblical study, encouraging them to discover the gems of universal truth that lie in the details of God's Word. When questions appear difficult or unclear, the Leaders Guide provides a doorway to the answers. "Applying the Message" leads participants from the recorded Word of God to its possible application in our present lives. It helps participants more fully realize the implications of God's Word for their daily experience as a Christian. Finally, "Taking the Message Home" invites participants to continue their scriptural meditation at home. Suggestions are given for personal reflection, for preview of the following session, and for private study of topics raised by the session. The study of God's Word will be greatly enhanced by those actively pursuing the suggestions offered in this section.

Each session ends with some trivia that is intended to spark interest and generate additional discussion. This can be used to develop inquisitiveness and enthusiasm about related issues ripe for exploration.

A glossary is provided at the end of the Study Guide. Because a study of the Bible will lead participants to language that may occasionally seem foreign and difficult, the glossary will make participants more comfortable with unfamiliar terms, phrases, and customs. The glossary will help them understand biblical concepts such as love and grace, whose definitions may differ from current definitions.

The Bible study also includes easy-to-read charts and interesting illustrations that will aid participants in their understanding of biblical concepts and history. These should be referred to frequently as they give visual support to the context of the sessions.

Session 1

The Sad State of the World

(Romans 1)

Approaching This Study

What a wonderful experience we have ahead of us! Of all the books of the Bible, perhaps none other expresses God's plan of salvation as clearly as Paul's letter to the Romans. Romans systematically constructs an image of our world's sinful condition, then details God's plan to redeem, or "buy back," people from the hopelessness of their sinful state. If you desire an understanding of the relationship between the two main doctrines of the Bible—Law and Gospel—reading Romans is essential. When we have completed this study, we will have a much greater understanding of God's incredible, gracious intervention in our lives.

Paul probably wrote this letter, or epistle, to the Christian church worshiping in Rome. Most of its members were Gentiles (that is, non-Jews), although a sizable minority were of Jewish origin. Some friction had arisen between the Gentile Christians and the Jewish Christians, causing Paul to delineate their relationship in God's overall plan of redemption. Unlike many of the churches to which Paul wrote, this Christian community had not yet been visited by the apostle. So Paul hoped to construct for them a basic understanding of the Gospel message, laying a foundation for his upcoming visit. He also hoped to gain support for his proposed mission outreach into Spain. Paul wrote this letter from the city of Corinth, in the country we call Greece today, in early spring of A.D. 57, less than 30 years after Jesus was crucified, rose from the dead, and ascended into heaven.

Let's approach this study with thanksgiving for the unparalleled gift God has granted us through the death of His only Son. We were lost in our sins. But God's love for us was so great He would not allow us to perish. He had a plan. And the plan worked.

An Overview

Unit Reading

Divide the reading of this first chapter into three parts. After reading Romans 1:1–7, summarize its main points. Do the same after reading Romans 1:8–17 and again after reading Romans 1:18–32. What foundational points does Paul construct in this first chapter?

The Message in Brief

Paul begins this letter by introducing himself and his credentials. In doing so, he exposes his readers to such important concepts as apostleship, sainthood, Old Testament prophecy, the two natures of Jesus Christ, election, and sanctification. These will be explored in the upcoming section.

In typical fashion, Paul praises those Christians in Rome who have steadfastly remained faithful to Jesus Christ. He expresses his desire to visit so that he and the Roman Christians may enjoy mutual support and edification. Finally, Paul presents the theme of his letter: "the righteous will live by faith."

Having completed his opening remarks, Paul sketches the sinful nature of the world's Gentile population. They have lived in a constant state of rebellion against God, causing Him to abandon them to the consequences of their sin. In the next chapter, Paul will summarize the sins of the Jews, and in the third chapter, he will review the sins prevalent among both the Jews and the Gentiles. By engaging in this discussion, Paul emphasizes sin's dire consequences for all people. These consequences could only be reversed by the sacrifice of God's only Son on the cross.

Working with the Text

Introduction (Romans 1:1–7)

1. Look up the word *apostle* in a Bible dictionary. How would you describe Paul as an apostle? Compare an apostle to a missionary or an evangelist.

2. One of the miraculous and mysterious aspects of Jesus is that, though one person, He has two natures. He is both human and divine at the same time. According to Paul's introduction, how was Jesus' human nature manifested? How was His divine nature manifested?

3. Paul describes some of the Romans as having been "called" to belong to Jesus Christ. Read Ephesians 1:4–14 and expand your understanding of what it means to be called by Christ.

When were we chosen? What does God grant us as His chosen? What has God given as a seal to prove we have been called? Now read Ephesians 2:8–10. For what purpose has God created us? When we are given the gift of faith, we naturally respond by wanting to serve God in good works. This process of following God is sometimes called sanctification. How does this relate to the purpose for our call according to Romans 1:5?

> For He chose us in Him before the creation of the world to be holy and blameless in His sight. In love He predestined us to be adopted as His sons through Jesus Christ, in accordance with His pleasure and will—to the praise of His glorious grace, which He has freely given us in the One He loves. In Him we have redemption through His blood, the forgiveness of sins, in accordance with the riches of God's grace that He lavished on us with all wisdom and understanding. And He made known to us the mystery of His will according to His good pleasure, which He purposed in Christ, to be put into effect when the times will have reached their fulfillment—to bring all things in heaven and on earth together under one head, even Christ.

> In Him we were also chosen, having been predestined according to the plan of Him who works out everything in conformity with the purpose of His will, in order that we, who were the first to hope in Christ, might be for the praise of His glory. And you also were included in Christ when you heard the word of truth, the gospel of your salvation. Having believed, you were marked in Him with a seal, the promised Holy Spirit, who is a deposit guaranteeing our inheritance until the redemption of those who are God's possession—to the praise of His glory. Ephesians 1:4–14

For it is by grace you have been saved, through faith—and this not from yourselves, it is the gift of God—not by works, so that no one can boast. For we are God's workmanship, created in Christ Jesus to do good works, which God prepared in advance for us to do. Ephesians 2:8–10

4. The Gospel refers to everything in the Bible that points to Jesus' sacrificial death on the cross for our forgiveness and eternal life. According to verse 2, when was the Gospel first promised?

5. Notice Romans 1:7. Who are the "saints"? Is Paul referring to a few selected "super Christians"?

Paul's Desire to Visit Rome (Romans 1:8–17)

1. Why is Paul unashamed of the Gospel?

2. To whom did God first offer His salvation (see v.16)?

3. In the Old Testament, the people of Israel were chosen by God over all nations of the world to reflect His light and glory. This explains Jesus' initial ministry to the Jews of Palestine. Later, He ministered to the Gentiles of Samaria, Phoenicia, and the Decapolis. What is clear about whom God desires to save?

4. One reason Paul wants to visit the Roman Christians is to offer and receive moral and spiritual support. Another reason can be found in Romans 15:23–24. What is that reason?

The Sinful State of the Gentiles (Romans 1:18–32)

1. Some people wonder why God doesn't simply reveal Himself in the heavens one night, shouting "Here I am!" According to Paul, how has God already made His existence known to everyone?

2. Rather than acknowledge the existence of the true God, to what have people turned? Can you give contemporary examples of people "worshiping" things other than God?

3. As a result of the world's idolatry, God has allowed people to suffer the consequences of following false religions and gods. According to verses 24–27, what is one such consequence that is the result of people acting out their sinful desires? What are some additional consequences (vv. 28–32)?

Applying the Message

1. Paul claims he is not ashamed of the Gospel. That is noble, indeed! Have you ever demonstrated an "ashamed of the Gospel" attitude? If you feel comfortable doing so, discuss your moment of weakness with other members. Be aware that everyone has failed in this area at some point. Jesus' death on the cross won forgiveness for all sins, including our sinful failures to confess Jesus Christ as Lord.

2. Gay rights is a hot topic in America today. But remember what Paul says about such activity in this chapter. When people continually disobey God's will (because they no longer worship the true God, but rather, follow false philosophies), God will finally allow them their way, even as they face eternal destruction because of their sinful actions. Sadly, how do you see the truth of Paul's words being demonstrated today?

3. Notice, however, other consequences of idolatry include such sins as greed, envy, strife, deceit, gossiping, slander, disobedience, and so forth. What does this suggest about our attitude toward individuals who practice homosexuality? Should we view their behavior as any more atrocious than those who fail in these other ways?

4. Are some of Paul's writings difficult to understand already? Cheer up! You are not alone. What does Peter—Paul's friend and coworker—say about Paul's writings in 2 Peter 3:16–17? According to Peter, how can people use difficult-to-understand passages for their own negative purposes?

Taking the Message Home

Review

Take a recent newspaper and clip articles that present the most repulsive examples of sin in the world. Be prepared to share these examples with others in the group. Be careful to share only the facts and not to gossip about specific people or groups.

Looking Ahead

Read Romans 2:1–3:8. Much of this reading might seem puzzling, but write down what you believe Paul is saying. If there are passages that appear puzzling and difficult, jot them down.

Working Ahead

Complete one or more of the following suggestions before the next session:

1. What examples can you give of people who consider their nation or ethnic group superior to others? How might this narrow-mindedness be a symptom of sin's blindness? Contemplate the disastrous consequences bigotry and intolerance have played in world history. How do these attitudes continue to bring distress to people today?

2. Look up *Paul* in a Bible dictionary and read about his adventurous life. What strikes you most about his relationship with the Lord? In what ways does his life contrast with the lives of those who claim life's goal is to "eat, drink, and be merry"?

3. Look at the map of Rome from Paul's day and notice where each of the following were located: the Tiber River, the Forum, the Via Appia, and the Imperial Palaces. List the various temples existing within the city and the gods or goddesses to whom they were dedicated.

Did You Know . . .

The apostle Paul was born and raised a Jew. In fact, he was trained to be a disciplined Pharisee, one of those individuals who placed ultimate importance on following God's ceremonial and moral laws. As a zealous Jew, Paul was deeply involved in the first persecutions of the Christian church. He was instrumental in the death of the first Christian martyr, Stephen. In one of God's most remarkable acts of grace (undeserved love), He converted Paul to Christianity. As Paul rode to Damascus—intent on persecuting the Christians there—the risen and glorified Jesus appeared in blazing light and transformed the murdering unbeliever into a follower and servant of the Lord. Paul became the greatest Christian missionary in history. Truly, Paul could relate to the words, "Amazing grace! How sweet the sound that saved a wretch like me! I once was lost but now am found, was blind but now I see!"

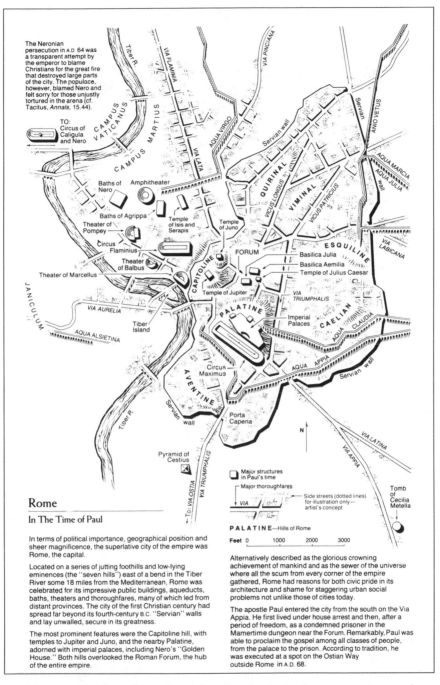

The Neronian persecution in A.D. 64 was a transparent attempt by the emperor to blame Christians for the great fire that destroyed large parts of the city. The populace, however, blamed Nero and felt sorry for those unjustly tortured in the arena (cf. Tacitus, *Annals*, 15.44).

TO: Circus of Caligula and Nero

Tiber R.

VIA FLAMINIA

VIA PINCIANA

CAMPUS VATICANUS

CAMPUS MARTIUS

CAMPUS LATA

VIA FLAMINIA

VIA LATA

AQUA VIRGO

Servian wall

ANIO VETUS

AQUA MARCIA

AQUA JULIA

QUIRINAL

VICUS LONGUS

VIMINAL

VICUS PATRICIUS

Servian wall

Baths of Nero

Amphitheater

Baths of Agrippa

Theater of Pompey

Temple of Isis and Serapis

Temple of Juno

Circus Flaminius

Theater of Balbus

Theater of Marcellus

CAPITOLINE

FORUM

ESQUILINE

VIA LABICANA

Basilica Julia

Basilica Aemilia

Temple of Julius Caesar

Temple of Jupiter

VIA TRIUMPHALIS

JANICULUM

VIA AURELIA

Tiber Island

PALATINE

Imperial Palaces

CAELIAN

AQUA CLAUDIA

AQUA ALSIETINA

Circus Maximus

AQUA APPIA

Servian wall

AVENTINE

Tiber R.

Servian wall

Porta Capena

N

VIA LATINA

VIA APPIA

Pyramid of Cestius

VIA TRIUMPHALIS

TO: VIA OSTIA

Major structures in Paul's time

Major thoroughfares

Side streets (dotted lines) for illustration only— artist's concept

VIA

Tomb of Cecilia Metella

PALATINE—Hills of Rome

Feet 0   1000   2000   3000

Rome

In The Time of Paul

In terms of political importance, geographical position and sheer magnificence, the superlative city of the empire was Rome, the capital.

Located on a series of jutting foothills and low-lying eminences (the "seven hills") east of a bend in the Tiber River some 18 miles from the Mediterranean, Rome was celebrated for its impressive public buildings, aqueducts, baths, theaters and thoroughfares, many of which led from distant provinces. The city of the first Christian century had spread far beyond its fourth-century B.C. "Servian" walls and lay unwalled, secure in its greatness.

The most prominent features were the Capitoline hill, with temples to Jupiter and Juno, and the nearby Palatine, adorned with imperial palaces, including Nero's "Golden House." Both hills overlooked the Roman Forum, the hub of the entire empire.

Alternatively described as the glorious crowning achievement of mankind and as the sewer of the universe where all the scum from every corner of the empire gathered, Rome had reasons for both civic pride in its architecture and shame for staggering urban social problems not unlike those of cities today.

The apostle Paul entered the city from the south on the Via Appia. He first lived under house arrest and then, after a period of freedom, as a condemned prisoner in the Mamertime dungeon near the Forum. Remarkably, Paul was able to proclaim the gospel among all classes of people, from the palace to the prison. According to tradition, he was executed at a spot on the Ostian Way outside Rome in A.D. 68.

Session 2

The Jewish Christians, Too, Are Sinners

(Romans 2:1–3:8)

Approaching This Study

Having determined the depth of the Gentiles' depravity in the first chapter, Paul now turns to the Jews. It is one thing for pagans to worship a false god because of their ignorance, but it is quite another for Jews—who possess the Law of God—to judge and look down upon others for breaking God's Law while they themselves break that same Law! As much as Paul condemned the pagan Gentiles for their idolatrous and perverted ways, Paul must condemn the Jews for their hypocrisy.

Jewish Christians, although looking to Jesus for their salvation, continued to insist on following the Old Testament ceremonial laws of God, while scorning the Gentile Christians' unwillingness to follow such laws. This conflict was persistent in the early Christian church. See how the conflict was addressed in each of the following passages:

Galatians 2:11–16

Colossians 2:16–17

Acts 11:2–3

Acts 10:45

Paul addressed the arrogance and hypocrisy of the Jewish Christians so that they, too, would recognize their failings, join with their Gentile brethren in all humility, and seek together the gift of unity in God's grace.

This session will help us better understand the use and abuse of God's Law. The Jews had lived with the belief that they could redeem themselves by strictly following all of God's laws. In fact, the Jews supplemented these laws with a host of other man-made laws devised to protect them from breaking God's Law. Paul hoped to dispel the illusion that one could base one's hope of salvation on following the Law. Whether Jew or Gentile, all sin and fall short of the glory of God. All people desperately need God's forgiving grace.

An Overview

Unit Reading

This can be a very difficult section of Romans to read. Paul's argument is sophisticated and his writing is difficult to follow at times. Read Romans 2:1–3:8. Then use the "Working with the Text" questions to gain a fuller understanding of Paul's teachings.

The Message in Brief

Many of the Jewish Christians were passing judgment on their Gentile Christian brothers and sisters. The Jewish Christians claimed believers in Christ had to follow many Old Testament ceremonial laws, including circumcision. Look up *circumcision* in a Bible dictionary. What does it have to say?

Paul reminded the Jewish Christians that those who wished to find redemption under the Law must follow perfectly that Law. If a person breaks just one law, that person is judged and eternally condemned. As a means of gaining salvation, then, circumcision is useless. It provides only an outward sign of what the Spirit of God must work in us inwardly, that is, a transformation of the heart and mind from unbelief to trust in God's plan of salvation. In this way, Paul at first seemed to discount the value of Judaism and its traditions. But he concluded that there *is* value in possessing a Jewish background because the Jews were the first to receive the Word of God.

17

Working with the Text

Paul Condemns Hypocritical Judging (Romans 2:1–16)

1. Webster's Third International Dictionary defines a hypocrite as "one who pretends to be what he is not or to have principles or beliefs that he does not have, esp., someone who falsely assumes an appearance of virtue or religion." Paul accuses the Jewish Christians of hypocrisy in verses 1–4. They presented themselves as models of right living because they claimed to observe Old Testament Law more faithfully than the Gentile Christians. According to verse 3, when people criticize and look down on others for behavior they themselves do, how does God react?

2. When Jesus returns to judge the world, who will be condemned first according to verses 9–10? And who will receive their eternal reward first? What makes a person a spiritual "Jew," according to Paul in Galatians 3:29?

> If you belong to Christ, then you are Abraham's seed, and heirs according to the promise. Galatians 3:29

3. To the confusion of some in the Christian church today, several passages of Scripture seem to suggest that one is given eternal life as a result of doing good works and obeying God's Law. How does Romans 2:7 seem to support this? But, how do the following passages refute this claim?

> This righteousness from God comes through faith in Jesus Christ to all who believe. There is no difference, for all have sinned and fall short of the glory of God, and are justified freely by His grace through the redemption that came by Christ Jesus. ... Where, then, is boasting? It is excluded. On what principle? On that of observing the law? No, but on that of faith. For we maintain that a man is justified by faith apart from observing the law. Romans 3:22–24, 27–28

For it is by grace you have been saved, through faith—and this not from yourselves, it is the gift of God—not by works, so that no one can boast. For we are God's workmanship, created in Christ Jesus to do good works, which God prepared in advance for us to do. Ephesians 2:8–10

We who are Jews by birth and not "Gentile sinners" know that a man is not justified by observing the law, but by faith in Jesus Christ. So we, too, have put our faith in Christ Jesus that we may be justified by faith in Christ and not by observing the law, because by observing the law no one will be justified. Galatians 2:15–16

You foolish man, do you want evidence that faith without deeds is useless? … You see that [Abraham's] faith and his actions were working together [when he offered his son Isaac on the altar], and his faith was made complete by what he did. James 2:20, 22

When passages taken out of context seem to contradict each other, it is important to look at other passages of Scripture to help explain the apparent contradiction. Passages like James 2:20, 22 help us understand how genuine faith in Jesus will manifest itself in good deeds and obedience to God's Law. Just as an apple tree naturally produces apples, a person with genuine faith will naturally produce good works. Good works are not a way to earn salvation, but they are evidence of the faith in Jesus that God gives us and through which He saves us. So, when Paul states that people who persistently do good works will obtain eternal life, he's simply recognizing how good deeds are evidence of genuine faith.

4. If an individual is unaware of God's Law, will that person be spared judgment (Romans 2:12)? God gave the people of Israel His Law in the Ten Commandments. Many Gentiles (non-Jews) lived and died without the benefit of that written Law. But how was much of God's Law understood by the Gentiles according to verse 14?

What Makes a True Jew? (Romans 2:17–29)

1. Apparently many of the Jewish Christians bragged that their solid relationship with the Lord was based on their knowledge of and obedience to God's Law. With what three examples does Paul illustrate their hypocrisy?

2. Whom would God prefer: someone who was circumcised and broke His Law, or someone who was not circumcised but obeyed His Law? What does that imply about the significance of circumcision?

3. Paul claims circumcision should not be merely "outward and physical," but rather, "inward" and "of the heart." Read Colossians 2:11–12. How do these verses explain Paul's reasoning in Romans 2:25–29?

> In Him you were also circumcised, in the putting off of the sinful nature, not with a circumcision done by the hands of men but with the circumcision done by Christ, having been buried with Him in Baptism and raise with Him through your faith in the power of God, who raised Him from the dead. Colossians 2:11–12

God's Faithfulness (Romans 3:1–8)

1. In some ways, Paul seems to devalue the importance of being a Jew, but in verses 2–3 he indicates there is great advantage to belonging to God's chosen people. What is one special gift the Jews have received

above and beyond the Gentiles? The rest of their benefits are listed later in Romans 9:4–5. What are they?

2. Even though many Jews had forsaken God by rejecting His promises, what does Paul confess about God's faithfulness in Romans 3:3–6?

3. There were some Christians in Rome who argued that the more sinful people behaved, the more God's holiness could be exalted. So, the greater the sin, the more God is glorified! Some even claimed Paul taught that people should deliberately sin so that Christ's grace and forgiveness could be magnified. What does Paul say about this kind of reasoning? How is this argument echoed in Romans 6:1–2?

Applying the Message

1. Some Christians today argue the most important aspect of faith is found in piety and virtue. In other words, one cannot be considered truly Christian unless one exhibits certain "right" behaviors—for example, abstaining from drinking, demonstrating a public prayer life, giving large amounts to charity, and speaking in tongues. How could you use the example of the Jewish Christians in Rome to refute this claim?

2. Some people refuse to attend church because they claim hyp-

ocrites are found there. In what ways are they right? In what sense are all Christians hypocrites? Why must this sad reality not prevent us from regularly joining with others in worship?

3. Paul seems to suggest that an individual's conscience reflects the Law of God. Most people have an innate "feeling" for what is right and wrong. Since most of the world is not Jewish or Christian, why is this a good thing? In what way does the Law of God help maintain social order? Read 1 Timothy 1:9–10 and explain one particular use of the Law.

> We also know that law is made not for the righteous but for lawbreakers and rebels, the ungodly and sinful, the unholy and irreligious; for those who kill their fathers or mothers, for murderers, for adulterers and perverts, for slave traders and liars and perjurers—and for whatever else is contrary to the sound doctrine. 1 Timothy 1:9–10

Taking the Message Home

Review

Meditate on Romans 2:25–29. Notice again how the Jewish rite of circumcision did not make a person a Jew in and of itself, but acted as a sign of something that was to happen on a spiritual level. It was a sign of God's Spirit working within an individual, bringing that person under the umbrella of God's promises. What does that mean about all Christians who have been given God's Spirit? In what sense have we all become Jews?

Looking Ahead

Read Romans 3:9–4:25 before the next session. In your own words, write the difference between receiving righteousness under the Law and receiving righteousness through faith in Jesus Christ. Can anyone be righteous under the Law? How are we made righteous through faith in Jesus Christ?

Working Ahead

Complete one or more of the following suggestions before the next session:

1. Read Genesis 15:1–7 and examine God's two most important promises to Abraham. What were they? What was it about Abraham's response to God's promises that made Abraham righteous in God's eyes? How would this apply to our response to the promise given in John 3:16?

2. Paul makes it clear no one can follow God's Law perfectly. All people break it frequently. The only one who kept the Law perfectly was Jesus Christ. If God's Law is so impossibly difficult to follow, why should it have any value for us today?

3. What makes a gift a gift? When someone gives us something of equal value to what we have given him or her, is it a gift? What differentiates a gift from a payback, or compensation, or a reward? What does it mean, then, when Christians say salvation is God's gift to us?

Did You Know . . .

Many of the Old Testament books are filled with a list of God's laws. But they are not always the same kind of laws. Some of them are moral laws, involving the way we treat each other and relate to God. Others are political laws that helped Israel establish its social order. And there are a host of ceremonial laws, involving ways of worshiping, offering sacrifices, and observing holy days. God's laws were difficult to follow, and the Jews made it worse by constructing much more complex laws designed to prevent people from attempting to break God's laws. In a way, these extra laws were like a "fence" to protect people from inadvertently trespassing. So, some rather ridiculous man-made laws were invented. For example, in order to prevent people from breaking God's command to rest on the Sabbath, people could not cut their fingernails, nor walk more than a thousand feet from their homes, nor harvest any of their fields on the Sabbath. Even healing the sick on the Sabbath was generally prohibited.

Session 3

God Makes Us "Right" through Faith

(Romans 3:9–4:25)

Approaching This Study

In this section of Scripture, Paul begins to outline the differences between the Law of God, which condemns us because of our sin, and the Gospel message of forgiveness through faith in Jesus Christ. After having condemned the Gentile pagans for their sinfulness and the Jews for theirs, Paul reiterates the sad fact that *all* people sin and fall short of God's will. He shows how God proclaimed the universal nature of sin in the writings of the Old Testament. But Paul also shares God's alternate method of salvation—apart from keeping the Law—won by the death and resurrection of Jesus Christ. Through faith in Jesus' sacrifice for our sins, God grants us forgiveness and eternal life.

An Overview

Unit Reading

Read Romans 3:9–4:25. Pause after each paragraph and identify Paul's main thought.

The Message in Brief

Paul hammers home the reality of sin's universal presence. It afflicts all people with devastating consequences. No one can make himself or herself "right" with God by following the Law. But, thanks be to God, He has offered us another way to reach our heavenly home. God took our sins and punished His own Son on the cross for them. In return, God provides us Jesus' innocence. God offers this gift to all people, but only some receive the faith to believe in His gift. Others reject it. Abraham is a classic example of someone who enjoyed the blessings of God after believing His promises. Abraham did not earn God's favor by being a good person. Rather, God declared Abraham righteous as a result of his faith in God's promises. God offers His gift of righteousness through faith in Jesus Christ to all people, Jews and Gentiles.

Working with the Text

All People Are Sinful (Romans 3:9–20)

1. Romans 3:19 says the Law speaks "so that every mouth may be silenced and the whole world held accountable to God." What picture does Paul create here? Why do people need to be silenced through the Law? How do you think the Law is able to accomplish this powerful feat?

2. In Romans 3:10–18 Paul combines a number of Old Testament passages to demonstrate the world's universal sinfulness. Read these Old Testament passages and compare them to the quotations given by Paul: Psalm 14:3; Ecclesiastes 7:20; Psalm 5:9; Psalm 140:3; Psalm 10:7; Isaiah 59:7–8; and Psalm 36:1. How would you describe the method by which Paul uses the Old Testament to support his contention? Do you think this use of the Old Testament was directed primarily toward the Gentile Christians or the Jewish Christians? Why?

All have turned aside, they have together become corrupt; there is no one who does good, not even one. Psalm 14:3

There is not a righteous man on earth who does what is right and never sins. Ecclesiastes 7:20

Not a word from their mouth can be trusted; their heart is filled with destruction. Their throat is an open grave; with their tongue they speak deceit. Psalm 5:9

They make their tongues as sharp as a serpent's; the poison of vipers is on their lips. Psalm 140:3

His mouth is full of curses and lies and threats; trouble and evil are under his tongue. Psalm 10:7

Their feet rush into sin; they are swift to shed innocent blood. Their thoughts are evil thoughts; ruin and destruction mark their ways. The way of peace they do not know; there is no justice in their paths. They have turned them into crooked roads; no one who walks in them will know peace. Isaiah 59:7–8

An oracle is within my heart concerning the sinfulness of the wicked: There is no fear of God before his eyes. Psalm 36:1

3. We've considered how the Law is a valuable tool to maintain order in God's world, helping restrain people from committing criminal acts. The Law of God serves another purpose as well. Of what use is God's Law according to Romans 3:20? How is this confirmed by Paul in Romans 7:7?

God Makes Us Righteous through Faith (Romans 3:21–31)

1. Original sin is the sin passed down from generation to generation since the time of Adam and Eve. If a person could be born without original sin and lead a life that kept God's Law perfectly, that person could, theoretically, earn his or her own salvation. But, of course, in the real world, such an accomplishment is impossible. Fortunately, God has offered another avenue to salvation. How does righteousness come to people according to verse 22? Is this avenue to salvation something we earn, or is it something freely given (see v. 24)?

2. God is holy, that is, without sin. And He is a just God. Because He is both holy and just, God must, by His very nature, exercise His justice against the world's sins. But who has received and accepted this justice and judgment according to verses 25–26? Who has suffered for the sins of the world? Now read 2 Corinthians 5:21 and Romans 4:25. Explain how Jesus' death on the cross grants us eternal life.

God made Him who had no sin to be sin for us, so that in Him we might become the righteousness of God. 2 Corinthians 5:21

He was delivered over to death for our sins and was raised to life for our justification. Romans 4:25

3. Can anyone really boast about her or his goodness before God? Why not? How does God bring us salvation? In other words, since Jesus has died for our sins, what does God work through so that we gain forgiveness and eternal life? Some might think, "Well, I may not be able to boast about how good I am, but I can sure boast about how strong my faith is!" Why is this no reason to boast according to Ephesians 2:8–9?

For it is by grace you have been saved, through faith—and this not from yourselves, it is the gift of God—not by works, so that no one can boast. Ephesians 2:8–9

4. Paul describes another purpose for God's Law in this section of Scripture. He mentions it in Romans 3:31. Also look up Romans 6:15–18 and explain your understanding of what theologians often call the "Third Use of the Law."

Abraham Made Righteous through Faith (Romans 4)

1. Abraham was considered the "father" of the Jews. So it is no mystery why Paul selected Abraham as the ultimate example of gaining righteousness through faith. His example would have a great impact on the Jewish Christians in Rome. Nonetheless, Paul wanted both the Jews and the Gentiles in the Roman church to understand their relationship to Abraham. After reading Romans 4:16–17 explain how all believers are heirs of Abraham.

2. It seems unnatural for us to "get something for nothing." But isn't that exactly how Paul explains the gift of salvation? Look at Romans 4:4–5 and state in your own words the illustration he uses to describe God's grace.

3. Abraham's faith was credited by God as righteousness even before Abraham was circumcised. Remember, circumcision was the Jews' ultimate sign of their separate identity as the people of God. But Paul points out how Abraham was given God's righteousness *before* he was circumcised. He remained righteous—through faith—after he was circumcised as well. How does this create an ingenious argument that both Jews and Gentiles are saved through faith and not by works (vv. 10–12)?

Applying the Message

1. How do you think a person's perspective of the world would be

altered if he or she understood its universal sinfulness? Is there any hope for a perfect, utopian society as some have hoped for in history? Will there ever be a perfect role model for people (besides, of course, Jesus Christ)? Is it legitimate to look to other cultures or societies either in the present or the past and glamorize them as somehow noble and ideal? Without God's forgiveness and promise of salvation, is there really any hope for the world?

2. Consider this scenario: A woman does not see the need for baptizing her children or bringing them to church because she feels they are as good as any other children in her neighborhood. What flaw do you see in this thinking? What advice do you think Paul would give this woman?

3. What difference would it make in your life if you sincerely, genuinely, and consistently enjoyed each day trusting in the promises of God's forgiveness and guidance just as Abraham trusted in God's promises? True, our God-given faith in Jesus is essential to eternal salvation, but consider the difference such faith makes in our day-to-day existence as well. How does it affect your relationship with your spouse and children? How does it affect your attitude at work or at school? How does it affect your understanding of future goals?

Taking the Message Home

Review

Reflect again on the great doctrines proclaimed in this section of Scripture. What are the three uses of God's Law, and to whom do you think each use applies? How does God's Law differ from the Gospel? Look up the word *grace* in a Bible dictionary and write down how this word applies to Jesus' sacrificial death.

Looking Ahead

With your understanding of Law and Gospel, read through Romans 5–6. Notice the stark contrast between sin (which arises as a consequence of the Law) and grace (which is granted us as a result of Jesus' death and resurrection). What are the consequences of sin? But what does God's grace bring us? Why do those who have received forgiveness desire to keep God's Law?

Working Ahead

Complete one or more of the following suggestions before the next session:

1. Take a few minutes to read the account of Adam and Eve's fall found in Genesis 3. The consequence of their fall was the onslaught of original sin. The sin that afflicted Adam and Eve would be passed down to their children and to all generations. We are conceived and born with it. In the upcoming chapter Paul will focus on the tragic reality of sin. It is within everyone, and it ultimately kills everyone. With this understanding, what would the world be like without the knowledge of Jesus Christ?

2. Through Baptism, Paul writes, people's old lives of enmity and hostility toward God are put to death and new spiritual people arise who desire to trust and obey the Lord. Baptism is a momentous event! It indicates a radical life change. It is something to celebrate! If possible, determine the date of your Baptism and mark that date on a calendar. Then be prepared to celebrate its anniversary.

3. Consider this scenario: Someone comes to your door and offers you a check. On the check you see written, "Pay to the bearer … eternal life." It is signed by Jesus. If you endorsed this check and tried to cash it, what would this say about your faith? If you laughed, tore up the check, and went back to the living room to watch TV, what would this say about your faith? Why is faith important for receiving salvation?

Did You Know . . .

Abraham possessed great faith in God's numerous promises to him. The Lord promised to bring Abraham into an unknown land where he would be richly blessed; Abraham so strongly believed God's promise, he moved his entire household to the land of Canaan. God also promised Abraham that his innumerable descendants would one day possess the Promised Land of Canaan, even though Abraham and his wife were childless until she was 90 years old and he was 100! Then the Lord tested Abraham's faith by commanding Abraham to sacrifice Isaac, his only son. At the last moment, God spared the son and provided a substitute, a ram.

Abraham would not live to see his countless descendants conquer the Promised Land, yet to his dying day, Abraham believed God would be true to His promises. The promise was fulfilled generations later when Joshua led the people of Israel into Canaan, conquering its cities and destroying its peoples.

We, too, are called to trust in God's promises, some of which we will see fulfilled in our lifetime while others will not be fulfilled until we reach our heavenly home. We will see God protect us and guide us through our earthly existence. We will experience the peace and joy that comes from His forgiveness. But we will not see the promise of heavenly bliss completely fulfilled until we reach our eternal destination with the Lord. Until then, we live each day believing God will do—sooner or later—exactly what He promises to do.

From *The Doré Bible Illustrations*. By permission of Dover Publications, Inc.

Session 4

The Two Different Worlds of Sin and Grace

(Romans 5–6)

Approaching This Study

The most liberating aspect of Christianity is the realization that we don't have to try to make ourselves good enough to be accepted by God. God accomplishes that for us through faith in Jesus Christ. Unfortunately, throughout the history of the Christian church, some voices have claimed that God's forgiveness means we no longer need His Law. Since we are forgiven anyway, why be concerned with obedience? In Romans 5–6 Paul emphasizes the third use of the Law as a guide for Christian living. Although God does indeed forgive each and every one of our sins, our response to God's love and grace is the desire to obey. We enjoy the opportunity to follow His will not only because we recognize that it is life-giving, but also because we want to please God. Through our faith in Christ Jesus, the Law nourishes rather than drains; it upholds and restores rather than destroys. As you read these two chapters from Romans, consider again the great gifts God has given His people—forgiveness of sins and eternal life. Thanks be to God!

An Overview

Unit Reading

Read Romans 5–6.

The Message in Brief

Having explained how God grants salvation through faith rather than by good works, Paul fears his readers will devalue the importance of good works. Romans 5–6 is an effort to emphasize the Christian's desire for holiness. God paid for our souls through the very high price of His only Son's death on the cross. As a result of this purchase, God has brought us into a new life of grace and forgiveness. Through Baptism, our sinful nature was buried along with Jesus. Just as Jesus rose from the dead on Easter morning, so a new nature was resurrected in us through Baptism. If our sinful nature—with all of its destructive and deadly characteristics—has been put to death, why return to our sinful ways? Why not follow the urging of our new nature and seek thoughts and deeds that glorify God and help our neighbors? Although we will always fall short of perfection, Paul's argument is persuasive. Since we now have a new Master in Jesus Christ whose ways bring goodness and life, why not follow Him and discard our sinful past?

Working with the Text

The Joy of Being Reconciled to God (Romans 5:1–11)

1. When people are "made right" with God through faith in Jesus Christ, they can face suffering with hope. Paul says in verses 3–4: "We also rejoice in our sufferings, because we know that suffering produces perseverance; perseverance, character; and character, hope." How do you explain this process? How does suffering produce perseverance? How does perseverance build character? And how does character increase hope?

2. Only rarely do we hear about someone giving up his or her life for someone else. Occasionally we hear of a soldier who took a bullet for a companion or a parent who is sacrificing everything so that her or his child might enjoy a better life. God's sacrifice in Jesus Christ is even more astounding. What is it about Jesus' sacrifice that makes every other sacrificial act pale in comparison (vv. 6–8)? What does this suggest about the depth of God's love for us? How does Paul summarize the depth of God's love in Romans 8:37–39?

3. Notice how Paul explains we've been justified (made right in God's eyes) through Jesus' blood (v. 9). This is not the first such reference to the importance of blood in God's process of justification. Paul writes in Romans 3:25, "God presented Him [Jesus] as a sacrifice of atonement, through faith in His blood." Why is the blood so important? Consider a description of the high priest's role during the Old Testament animal sacrifices as described in Hebrews 9:7. Then read Exodus 12:12–13 and 24:3–8. Notice the importance of blood as a means through which God delivered people from His wrath and reconciled them to Him. Read Leviticus 17:11 and explain the significance of blood to God. How does this relate to the importance of Holy Communion as shared by Jesus in Matthew 26:27–28?

But only the high priest entered the inner room, and that only once a year, and never without blood, which he offered for himself and for the sins the people had committed in ignorance. Hebrews 9:7

On that same night I will pass through Egypt and strike down every firstborn—both men and animals—and I will bring judgment on all the gods of Egypt. I am the LORD. The blood will be a sign for you on the houses where you are; and when I see the blood, I will pass over you. No destructive plague will touch you when I strike Egypt. Exodus 12:12–13

When Moses went and told the people all the LORD's words and laws, they responded with one voice, "Everything the LORD has said we will do." Moses then wrote down everything the LORD had said.

He got up early the next morning and built an altar at the foot of the mountain and set up twelve stone pillars representing the twelve tribes of Israel. Then he sent young Israelite men, and they offered burnt offerings and sacrificed young bulls as fellowship offerings to the LORD. Moses took half of the blood and put it in bowls, and the other half he sprinkled on the altar. Then he took the Book of the Covenant and read it to the people. They responded, "We will do everything the LORD has said; we will obey."

Moses then took the blood, sprinkled it on the people and said, "This is the blood of the covenant that the LORD has made with you in accordance with all these words." Exodus 24:3–8

For the life of a creature is in the blood, and I have given it to you to make atonement for yourselves on the altar; it is the blood that makes atonement for one's life. Leviticus 17:11

Then He took the cup, gave thanks and offered it to them, saying, "Drink from it, all of you. This is My blood of the covenant, which is poured out for many for the forgiveness of sins." Matthew 26:27–28

Adam Brought Sin, but Jesus Brings Life (Romans 5:12–21)

1. Interestingly, before God gave the written Law to Moses on Mount Sinai, people were not accountable for breaking that Law (v. 13). This seems only fair, doesn't it? Should a law composed today be retroactively applied to behavior committed years ago? Of course not! But, Paul says, even though the Law was not given until the time of Moses, people who lived before Moses still died. Why do people die according to Romans 6:23? So, before the time of Moses, even though people were not condemned to die under the Law, of what were they still guilty (vv. 12, 14)?

2. Even as Adam's sin condemned the whole world, what did Jesus' sacrificial death and resurrection accomplish (vv. 15–19)?

3. Paul concludes, "The law was added so that the trespass might increase." What use of the Law does this suggest to you?

Death Is Buried, and We Rise with Christ (Romans 6:1–14)

1. What imagery does Paul use to describe Baptism? What happens to the "old sinner" when someone is baptized? And what new life emerges as a result of Baptism? According to Romans 5 and 6:1–7, why is it appropriate to call a person's sinful nature the Old Adam and a person's desire to trust and obey the Lord the New Adam?

2. Paul states, "The death [Jesus] died, He died to sin once for all" (v. 10). This is a loaded sentence! How many times did Jesus sacrifice Himself for the sins of the world? And for whom did He die?

Freed from Sin and Slaves to Righteousness (Romans 6:15–23)

1. A logical, albeit distorted, response to God's grace suggests we should deliberately sin so His grace and forgiveness might be offered in abundance! How does Paul respond to that argument?

2. Paul's description of the human condition suggests people will live in slavery either to sin or to righteousness. In a sense, there is no human freedom to go back and forth. Either evil or righteousness will master us. That's not to say we will no longer sin when we are slaves to righ-

teousness, but it does mean we will no longer be completely governed by the power of evil. Why does this imagery argue against the theory we should sin boldly and frequently so that God's grace might be poured out more abundantly?

Applying the Message

1. The Word of the Lord calls us to be baptized. Some churches pour water onto people's heads; others immerse them in a pool of water. Either method fulfills God's command. In what way does immersion more graphically illustrate the death of the Old Adam and the birth of the New Adam?

2. Paul writes in Romans 5:6, "You see, at just the right time, when we were still powerless, Christ died for the ungodly." Do you think Jesus was born at just the right time in history? Why or why not? How do you think He would have been received in our age?

3. Share with other participants an experience in your life when suffering produced perseverance and perseverance, character, all of which has given you greater hope and confidence in the Lord.

Taking the Message Home

Review

Is there someone for whom you would sacrifice your life? Why would you be willing to do so? Would you be willing to be executed in place of a stranger in prison who was sentenced to die? Reflect on God's incredible love for us. Although we were sinners, completely at war with a holy God, Jesus offered His life for us. Why would anyone do that?

Looking Ahead

Before the next session, read Romans 7. Picture in your mind two worlds—one governed by evil and death, the other governed by joy and life. If you lived in a perfect world of joy and life, would you like your world soiled by acts of hatred, injustice, and wickedness? God prefers such a perfect world, while we have often chosen the world of wickedness. He desperately wants to rescue us from our dreadful fate and has sacrificed His only Son for our deliverance. We are redeemed into a new world of God's holiness, and yet, like the child who tracks muddy footprints onto a clean kitchen floor, we keep tracking in remnants of our sinful, dead world. How do you feel about sin as you struggle in your present situation? As you grow in your knowledge of sin and grace, how will your perspective of God's glory and mercy increase?

Working Ahead

Complete one or more of the following suggestions before the next session:

1. Talk to someone who has remarried after the death of his or her spouse. Ask the person whether the transition to a second spouse was difficult or easy and what important differences he or she has found in the second marriage.

2. Review the Ten Commandments as outlined in Exodus 20:1–17. What surprised you most about these commandments after reading them again? Have you followed any of these commandments perfectly? What does that mean about your need for Christ?

3. In the privacy of your home, list some examples of the behaviors you strive to avoid but continue to commit. Bring these shortcomings to the Lord and ask for His forgiveness and for the strength to battle those sins. Isn't it frustrating how part of our consciousness hopes to avoid evil, while another part is attracted to it?

Did You Know . . .

According to Genesis 1:27, God created Adam and Eve in His own image. Adam and Eve were created with a perfect knowledge and will to follow God's Law.

They were holy even as God is holy. After eating the forbidden fruit of the tree of the knowledge of good and evil, Adam and Eve lost God's unique image. Their sons would inherit a different image, resulting in murder and death. Cain would kill his brother Abel. Notice how this sad reality is worded in Genesis 5:1–3: "When God created man, He made him in the likeness of God. He created them male and female and blessed them. And when they were created, He called them 'man.' When Adam had lived 130 years, he had a son *in his own likeness, in his own image* [italics added]; and he named him Seth." Seth inherited a fallen, sinful image, which continues to be handed down to all people today. The promise of Scripture is that through Baptism God restores His image. Sometimes that image is called the New Adam. When we die in the Lord, His image will be completed in us. What will it be like to be sinless in a world without sin?

The Law

Ten Commandments
Given at Mount Sinai

Exodus 20

The Gospel

Mount Calvary

John 3:16

Law and Gospel

Two Main Doctrines

The Bible is rightly "divided" into two main teachings: Law and Gospel.

These two doctrines stand out in t Bible like two mountain peaks.

The Difference between Lᶜ and Gospel

LAW

Tells what *we* are to do
Convicts us of sin
Preached to unrepentant sinners
Serves as a guide
for penitent believers

GOSPEL

Tells what *God* has done
Saves us
Preached to troubled sinners
Creates a living faith

Aid to Memory

LAW **S**hows	**O**ur	**S**in
GOSPEL **S**hows	**O**ur	**S**avior

The G-O-S-P-E-L in a sentence (also called "the Gospel-in-a-shell").

G od so loved the world that He gave His

O ne and only

S on, that whoever believes in Him shall ɪ

P erish but have

E ternal

L ife.

John 3:16

The word *Gospel* comes from the old English word *Godspell*.

Good news ⎫
Glad tidings ⎭ that Jesus is my Savior

Session 5

The Struggle against Sin

(Romans 7)

Approaching This Study

Paul has stressed the reality of sin to both the Gentile Christians and the Jewish Christians in Rome. But he doesn't simply point fingers at others. In this chapter, Paul points to himself and his own personal struggle with sin. For Paul, the temptation to sin is powerful, and his battle against sin is often unsuccessful. Of course, people have no need to struggle against sin until God's Law confronts them with its reality. That's one of the important purposes of God's Law. It demonstrates how far we fall short of following God's will. Were it not for the Law, we would rationalize away our sinful thoughts and behaviors or merely compare ourselves to others and contentedly conclude we are "relatively good." The Law of God, particularly as it is defined by Jesus during His Sermon on the Mount (Matthew 5), is broad and inclusive. No person can follow God's will perfectly. Fortunately, through Baptism, God's Spirit creates a new person in us, one who desires to trust and follow the Lord. Nonetheless, the sinful nature continues to battle the new nature in Christ. Even though we have received forgiveness and eternal life through Jesus' death and resurrection, temptations continue, and we all too often succumb to them. Release from this struggle will only be complete when we reach our heavenly home.

An Overview

Unit Reading

Using the New International Version of the Bible, read this chapter paragraph by paragraph. After reading each paragraph, try to summarize its main points.

The Message in Brief

After Paul continues his focus on the universal power of sin to bring death and destruction, he introduces an understanding of God's life-giving Gospel in Jesus Christ. Truly, believers will always struggle with sin because our sinful nature directs us away from God's will. But because of our new nature, given through God's Spirit, we no longer live under sin's dominion. Having condemned both the Jewish Christians and the Gentile Christians as sinners, Paul confesses his own inability to lead a perfectly God-pleasing life. He recognizes Jesus Christ as the only One who can deliver people from the struggle between good and evil.

Working with the Text

Released to Serve the Spirit (Romans 7:1–6)

1. What does God's Law indicate about His intent for the length of a marriage (Matthew 19:3–6; 1 Corinthians 7:10–11)? Does God condone divorce (Matthew 19:7–9)? Are there conditions under which the Lord has made an exception to marriage as a lifelong union? What are these two circumstances (Matthew 5:32; 1 Corinthians 7:15)?

Some Pharisees came to Him to test Him. They asked, "Is it lawful for a man to divorce his wife for any and every reason?"

"Haven't you read," He replied, "that at the beginning the Creator 'made them male and female,' and said, 'For this reason a man will leave his father and mother and be united to his wife, and the two will become one flesh'? So they are no longer two, but one. Therefore what God has joined together, let man not separate." Matthew 19:3–6

To the married I give this command (not I, but the Lord): A wife must not separate from her husband. But if she does, she must remain unmarried or else be reconciled to her husband. And a husband must not divorce his wife. 1 Corinthians 7:10–11

"Why then," they asked, "did Moses command that a man give his wife a certificate of divorce and send her away?" Jesus replied, "Moses permitted you to divorce your wives because your hearts were hard. But it was not this way from the beginning. I tell you that anyone who divorces his wife, except for marital unfaithfulness, and marries another woman commits adultery." Matthew 19:7–9

"But I tell you that anyone who divorces his wife, except for marital unfaithfulness, causes her to become an adulteress, and anyone who marries the divorced woman commits adultery." Matthew 5:32

But if the unbeliever leaves, let him do so. A believing man or woman is not bound in such circumstances; God has called us to live in peace. 1 Corinthians 7:15

2. When someone's spouse dies, the living spouse is free to marry someone else. How is this an illustration of what happens when we no longer seek salvation under the Law? If we are no longer "married" to the Law as a way to earn eternal life, to whom and what are we free to "marry" instead? Notice how Paul expands on the picture of God's people "marrying" Jesus Christ in Ephesians 5:22–33. Through what means does Jesus make His people holy in preparation for the marriage (Ephesians 5:26–27)?

Wives, submit to your husbands as to the Lord. For the husband is the head of the wife as Christ is the head of the church, His body, of which He is the Savior. Now as the church submits to Christ, so also wives should submit to their husbands in everything.

Husbands, love your wives, just as Christ loved the church and gave Himself up for her to make her holy, cleansing her by the washing with water through the word, and to present her to Himself as a radiant church, without stain or wrinkle or any other blemish, but holy and blameless. In this same way, husbands ought to love their wives as their own bodies. He who loves his wife loves himself. After all, no one ever hated his own body, but he feeds and cares for it, just as Christ does the church—for we are members of His body. "For this reason a man will leave his father and mother and be united to his wife, and the two will become one flesh." This is a profound mystery—but I am talking about Christ and the church. However, each one of you also must love his wife as he loves himself, and the wife must respect her husband. Ephesians 5:22–33

The Law Creates the Knowledge of Sin (Romans 7:7–13)

1. Look up the definition of *covet* in the dictionary and write it down. God's Law has informed us it is wrong to covet those things possessed by others. In what ways do you see this sin frequently committed in our society?

2. What does the Law do according to verses 7–8? Is it true that we would not know the meaning of sin were it not for the written Law or our conscience? Without such restraints, do you think we would be concerned about committing adultery or neglecting our worship of the Lord? Would we find anything objectionable about harmful gossip? How about fraud and deceit? What does the moral decay in our society suggest about people's awareness of God's Law and the sin that results from breaking it?

3. The Law was originally given to offer God's creatures a joyful, fulfilling life. It still serves such a purpose for believers in Christ who have received forgiveness and eternal life. But without God's grace in Jesus Christ, what would the Law bring, according to verse 10? Why?

The Inner Struggle between Good and Evil (Romans 7:14–25)

1. Is obedience to God's will easy? Describe in your own words the struggle Paul endured between his sinful desires and obedience to God's will.

2. Paul describes an ongoing battle between the "members of my body" and the "law of my mind." How would you describe this struggle? What two opposing forces are at work in our daily lives?

3. How does verse 25 express the existence of the Old Adam and the New Adam? How does it also support Paul's contention that we are either a slave to sin or a slave to righteousness? What is our only hope for resolving this confusing and frustrating situation?

Applying the Message

1. What is our response to God's love according to 1 John 4:11? How do we demonstrate love for God and one another according to 1 John 5:2–3? What motivates the Christian's obedience to God's will?

Dear friends, since God so loved us, we also ought to love one another. 1 John 4:11

This is how we know that we love the children of God: by loving God and carrying out His commands. This is love of God: to
obey His commands. 1 John 5:2–3

2. In a way, Paul defines the driving force behind sin as something
similar to what psychologists call an addiction or a compulsion. Paul says,
"I do not understand what I do. For what I want to do I do not do, but
what I hate I do. ... For what I do is not the good I want to do; no, the
evil I do not want to do—this I keep on doing." In our day and age, do
you think it is appropriate to say people have an "addiction" or "compulsion" to sin? Those who suffer from substance addiction or are
addicted to certain destructive behaviors discover that the first step
toward healing involves becoming aware of and recognizing the problem. In what similar manner does the Law function according to Paul?
Further healing from an addiction comes from sharing one's difficulties
with others who are plagued by the same problem. It is important to
admit the reality of the disease, confess its presence, and then make
amends to those who have been hurt. What similar actions happen in the
Christian church? Another important step in recovery involves proac-
tively helping others who are suffering from the same addiction. How
does the Lord call upon Christians to work in the same manner? In what
way might the local Christian congregation be considered a chapter of
"Sinners Anonymous"?

3. There are some Christian denominations that claim once we have
been saved, we no longer sin. How would you respond to their claims?

4. Paul says the Law only has authority over us while we live on this
earth. Why will the Law be irrelevant when we reach our heavenly

home? Can you even conceive of an existence without the presence of sin and evil? Read Revelation 21:3–4 and describe the blessings of a world without sin.

> And I heard a loud voice from the throne saying, "Now the dwelling of God is with men, and He will live with them. They will be His people, and God Himself will be with them and be their God. He will wipe every tear from their eyes. There will be no more death or mourning or crying or pain, for the old order of things has passed away." Revelation 21:3–4

Taking the Message Home

Review

We have pondered how God's Law convicts us of sin. Jesus, too, used the Law to convict His hearers of the depth and breadth of their sin. Look up Matthew 5:21–32 and notice how broadly the commandments of God extend into our lives. Can anyone live up to the Law?

Looking Ahead

As time permits, slowly read Romans 8. Write down the passages you find difficult to understand, and express in your own words the meanings of the passages you do understand.

Working Ahead

Complete one or more of the following suggestions before the next session:

1. Spend a few minutes contemplating the concept of eternity. Can you think of any illustration that might help define the length of eternity? What feelings does the prospect of living forever evoke? Consider the difficulties you currently face. How important are they when compared to an eternity with the Lord?

2. Must we always know exactly what we should pray for? Reflect on a situation where you were unable to formulate a prayer because you were uncertain which solution would be best. If possible, be ready to

share with others the outcome of your difficult experience. How did the Lord solve your problem?

3. If a person claims to have faith in the Lord Jesus but persistently and deliberately breaks God's Law in every possible manner, would you consider that person's faith genuine? Why or why not? Why is it impossible to claim faith in Jesus as Lord and Savior while continuing to live an intentionally sinful life? Be prepared to discuss these questions in the next session.

Did You Know . . .

What would life have been like had Adam and Eve never sinned? No one knows the answer to that intriguing question, but even Martin Luther contemplated the possibility. Consider one of his statements:

If Eve had not sinned, we would nonetheless have eaten, drunk, slept, etc., but all this without any sin and disorder. Such a life would have continued as long as it pleased God, let us say for two or three thousand years. Then we would have been changed in a moment without passing through death; and, completely sanctified, we would have entered into an eternal life free from trouble, such a life as, indeed, we are even now expecting. But because sin has stolen into the world through the work of the devil and the consent of man, the judgment has been passed from the beginning and remains in force throughout this life.

From Ewald M. Plass, compiler, *What Luther Says: An Anthology*, Vol. III, p. 1291. © 1959 CPH. All rights reserved.

According to Genesis 5, some of our early ancestors lived hundreds of years! But no matter how long they lived, they faced the prospect of death.

Sin_____

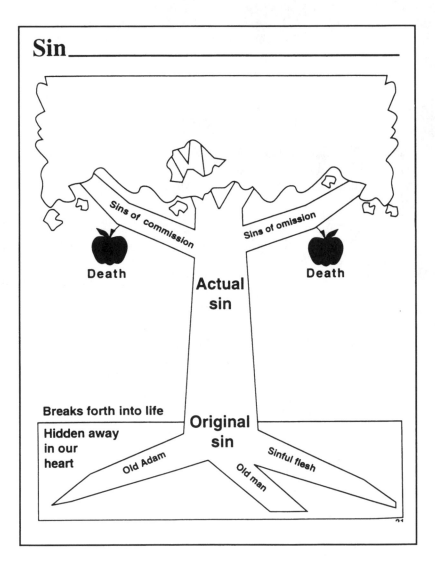

Sins of commission

Sins of omission

Death

Death

Actual sin

Breaks forth into life

Hidden away in our heart

Original sin

Old Adam

Old man

Sinful flesh

Session 6

Present Struggles Lead to Future Glory

(Romans 8)

Approaching This Study

When couples receive marital counseling because they have grown apart and no longer feel love for each other, the counselor will often require them to behave lovingly toward each other even though they do not feel in love. Interestingly, these loving acts, although initially not very sincere, usually lead to genuine feelings of love and affection. In other words, sometimes our hearts will follow where our actions lead. This is true with obedience to God's will. When we strive to follow God's will by seeking opportunities to hear and study His Word, the Holy Spirit strengthens our faith, enabling our hearts and minds to grow closer to Him.

All people have been infected with the fatal curse of sin. Whether Jew or Gentile, all will suffer death because of it. But there is final victory for those who receive Jesus Christ as their Savior from sin. In Romans 8, Paul continues to examine the ongoing struggle between the old sinful nature that afflicts people and the new spiritual life under the Lord that the Holy Spirit works in believers. There is no doubt about it: the battle between good and evil rages on in the hearts and minds of each Christian. By remaining connected to God's Word, we receive the Spirit's power as we struggle against sinful desires and strive to follow God's will. Without any help from us, God has freed us to live a new life controlled by His Spirit.

An Overview

Unit Reading

Read Romans 8:1–17 and discuss the two forces that struggle within the heart and mind of each Christian. Then read Romans 8:18–27. What are some examples of the way we witness creation "groaning" for deliverance? Finally, read Romans 8:28–39. What comfort does it bring to know the strength of God's love for us?

The Message in Brief

Having not only underscored the universal nature of sin, but also his own personal struggle with it, Paul reminds his readers of Jesus' victory over sin and death. As a result of Jesus' victory, we are given God's Spirit of life and peace. That Spirit dominates our lives. Because we have been removed from the world of sin and death and brought into a new world of life and peace, we desire to follow the ways of Him who won this new life for us. The old sinful nature will continue to struggle with the new nature, but in the end, glory will be ours through Jesus Christ. So, Paul calls on all believers to consciously and deliberately struggle against temptation, looking forward to the future glory God has promised. We can be certain God will be faithful to His promise because He tells us that nothing can separate us from His love in Christ Jesus.

Working with the Text

Controlled by the Spirit (Romans 8:1–17)

1. For whom is there no longer any condemnation? Notice the parallelism used by Paul to explain why this is so: "the law of the Spirit of life" has freed us from "the law of sin and death." Paul uses the word *law* in a number of different ways in Romans. When he mentions "the law of the Spirit of life," he is referring to the controlling power of the Holy Spirit. Knowing this, explain what Paul is saying in Romans 8:2.

2. Focus on verses 3 and 4. The Law can no longer save us because sin keeps us from fulfilling that Law. So, what did God do in order to bring us salvation? In what form did God send His Son? Read Leviticus 4:1–5 and explain the purpose of a sin offering. How did Jesus become such an offering? Perhaps the most interesting sentence in this chapter of Romans is found in verses 3b–4: "And so [God] condemned sin in sinful man, in order that the righteous requirements of the law might be fully met in us, who do not live according to the sinful nature but according to the Spirit." Some variations say, "And so He condemned sin in the

flesh …" Either way, who received the condemnation instead of us? How could Paul describe Jesus as "sinful man"? Wasn't Jesus sinless? Look up 2 Corinthians 5:21 to solve the riddle. How does this help us understand that through Jesus "the righteous requirements of the law might be fully met in us"?

The LORD said to Moses, "Say to the Israelites: 'When anyone sins unintentionally and does what is forbidden in any of the LORD's commands—

" 'If the anointed priest sins, bringing guilt on the people, he must bring to the LORD a young bull without defect as a sin offering for the sin he has committed. He is to present the bull at the entrance to the Tent of Meeting before the LORD. He is to lay his hand on its head and slaughter it before the LORD. Then the anointed priest shall take some of the bull's blood and carry it into the Tent of Meeting.' " Leviticus 4:1–5

3. Review Romans 8:5–11. There are two forces that can control us— either the sinful nature or the Spirit. Describe a person's relationship to the Lord when he or she is controlled by the sinful nature? When the person is controlled by the Spirit, how does that relationship change? After reading verse 10, describe what must happen to our bodies even though we are controlled by the Spirit. But what happens to our spirits?

4. If an individual is controlled by the Spirit, what will be his or her attitude toward sin? If we are controlled by the Spirit, Paul says, we are God's children. In this role, we share both Jesus' sufferings and glory. In what ways do you think a Christian will suffer simply because she or he is a Christian?

The Glory to Come (Romans 8:18–27)

1. Refer to Genesis 3:17–19. How was creation "subjected to frustration"? How does creation "feel" about this according to Romans 8:22? What hope do we have for our future?

To Adam He [God] said, "Because you listened to your wife and ate from the tree about which I commanded you, 'You must not eat of it,'

"Cursed is the ground because of you; through painful toil you will eat of it all the days of your life. It will produce thorns and thistles for you, and you will eat the plants of the field. By the sweat of your brow you will eat your food until you return to the ground, since from it you were taken; for dust you are and to dust you will return." Genesis 3:17–19

2. Throughout this earthly life, we groan in frustration as well. We long for our own eternal redemption. Often, in our weakness, we do not even know what to pray for. How does God's Spirit help in our predicament?

3. If someone could prove the existence of an afterlife with the Lord, would there be any need for faith? How does Paul state this simple truth in verse 24? How does Hebrews 11:1 support Paul's contention?

Now faith is being sure of what we hope for and certain of what we do not see. Hebrews 11:1

The Enduring Love of God (Romans 8:28–39)

1. In verse 29 Paul makes a powerful claim: believers in Christ were

chosen as God's children before the beginning of time. How does our predestined or predetermined status as God's children lead to our eventual glory, according to verse 30?

2. After reading verses 31–39, explain why believers in Christ need never fear the loss of God's love nor His abandonment.

3. According to verse 34, Jesus is still active. What does He continue to do for those who have received the gift of saving faith?

Applying the Message

1. In this chapter, Paul explains how a holy and just God, who must punish sin, could show us mercy and grace instead of condemnation. He took our sins and placed them on His Son. His Son then died for them. The innocence and righteousness upheld by the Son throughout His life was, at the same time, transferred to us. When God looks at us, He now sees the holiness of His Son. Wow! How does Paul's explanation help us understand what was happening to Jesus in Matthew 27:45–46? Describe what this tremendous sacrifice by the Lord means to you.

From the sixth hour until the ninth hour darkness came over all the land. About the ninth hour Jesus cried out in a loud voice, "*Eloi, Eloi, lama sabachthani?*"—which means, "My God, My God, why have You forsaken Me?" Matthew 27:45–46

2. Share with others in your group a moment when you were unable to pray because you had no understanding of what you should pray for. Why is it a relief to know the Spirit intercedes for us in such times and offers the right prayers to God? How might this understanding enable us to surrender our problems to the Lord?

3. Paul portrays an interesting picture of believers. Within each Christian are two driving forces competing for attention. One force would compel us to sin; the other would compel us to follow God's will. Although we have no innate power to make ourselves God's children, once the Holy Spirit has called us to faith, He motivates us to seek strength in God's Word. How might spending time in God's Word enable you to obey God's will and help you fight the compulsion to sin?

Taking the Message Home

Review

Reread Romans 8 and reflect on your personal struggle with good and evil. Under what circumstances are you most vulnerable to temptation? How might you be able to direct your thoughts or restructure your environment to resist such temptations? When we fail (as we frequently will), God's presence and love abide with us.

Looking Ahead

Read Romans 9 and focus particularly on verses 14–18. Taken out of context, these verses could be fearsome, suggesting God has predetermined some people to damnation. But why can't we make that claim, according to 1 Timothy 2:3–4 and John 3:17? Although God desires to save all people, some will reject Him. How can God's desire to save all people provide a tremendous comfort to those who love and follow the Lord?

Working Ahead

Complete one or more of the following suggestions before the next session:

1. The Bible occasionally refers to the "hardening of the heart." It is a term that describes people deliberately rejecting the Lord. Provide evidence that this occurs today.

2. Read parts of the story of Jacob and Esau. Refer to Genesis 25:21–34 and Genesis 27:1–40. Be ready to report on this story. Consider how Esau, as the firstborn, should have received the birthright and all the blessings of the firstborn, but Jacob received them instead. What is your feeling about this? Was this fair?

3. Reflect on those who uphold the Jewish faith. They have the promises of the Messiah found in the Old Testament, they look forward to the coming of the Messiah, but they refuse to recognize Jesus as the fulfillment of the promises and prophecies. In your opinion, why is it so difficult for them to confess Him as Lord? Despite all the prophecies that point directly to Jesus, why do some dismiss His person and work?

Did You Know . . .

Paul finally journeyed to Rome under the most difficult conditions. In around A.D. 58, Paul entered Jerusalem and began preaching. The Jews within the city incited a riot against him. Paul was taken into protective custody and was about to be flogged for his preaching when he claimed exemption due to his Roman citizenship. After Paul boldly and persuasively spoke to the Sanhedrin (the ruling religious authorities in Jerusalem), some 40 men vowed to fast until they had Paul killed. News of the plot reached the local Roman commander, and Paul was escorted to Caesarea to be interviewed by the Roman procurator named Felix. Felix, wanting to court favor with the Jews, simply left Paul in confinement. When the next procurator succeeded Felix, he wanted to return Paul to Jerusalem for trial, but Paul, according to his right as a Roman citizen, appealed to the emperor in Rome. The procurator had to abide by the appeal and sent an escort with Paul to Rome. The journey was harrowing, involving a shipwreck on the coast of Malta. When Paul finally arrived in Rome, he was allowed to rent a house and receive visitors even though he was guarded for two years under house arrest.

Whether Paul fulfilled his desire to reach Spain is uncertain. The fourth-century bishop of Caesarea, Eusebius, records Paul was taken again to Rome and killed during Nero's persecution in A.D. 67. The second-century "father of the African church," Tertullian, records that Paul was beheaded.

The Sacrificial Substitution

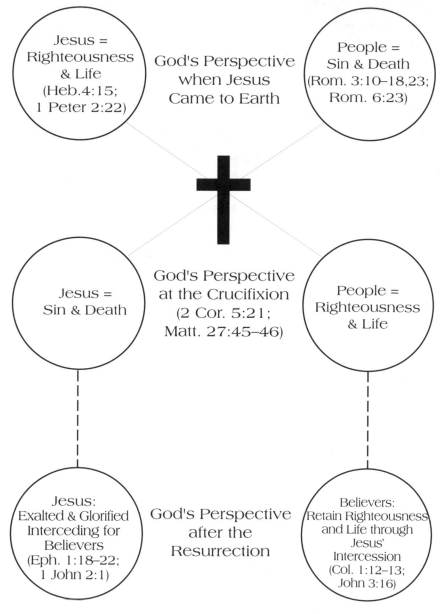

Jesus =
Righteousness
& Life
(Heb.4:15;
1 Peter 2:22)

God's Perspective
when Jesus
Came to Earth

People =
Sin & Death
(Rom. 3:10–18,23;
Rom. 6:23)

Jesus =
Sin & Death

God's Perspective
at the Crucifixion
(2 Cor. 5:21;
Matt. 27:45–46)

People =
Righteousness
& Life

Jesus:
Exalted & Glorified
Interceding for
Believers
(Eph. 1:18–22;
1 John 2:1)

God's Perspective
after the
Resurrection

Believers:
Retain Righteousness
and Life through
Jesus'
Intercession
(Col. 1:12–13;
John 3:16)

Session 7

Election

(Romans 9)

Approaching This Study

Why are some people saved while others are not? Paul approaches this deep and perplexing mystery in Romans 9. Just as He chose the people of Israel out of all the nations in the world to be His special nation, so He chooses (elects) those who will receive salvation in Jesus Christ. While we know from messages like 1 Timothy 2:4 that God desires all people to be saved and no one to be damned, some people reject His grace.

It breaks our heart to see a loved one reject the Lord. No matter what may be said or done, he or she may remain a staunch unbeliever. In the same way, Paul is crushed as he witnesses his own people, the Jews, rejecting Jesus. But he is encouraged by the number of Gentiles who receive what the Jews have rejected. Paul affirms that eternal life is not owed those who are Abraham's descendants, but rather, it is freely given to those who trust in Jesus as their Savior from sin. Knowing the Lord has chosen us for salvation, we praise and glorify God for His election. The fact that believers have received the Holy Spirit in Baptism and trust in Jesus for their salvation is evidence of their selection. And so, our understanding of God's election comforts us, gives us the conviction that we are indeed delivered from sin and death, and helps us know that we possess the sure promise of eternal life in God's heavenly kingdom.

An Overview

Unit Reading

Read Romans 9. Underline those verses that are difficult to understand. At the end of this session, review those verses that remain confusing and ask others in your group for their insights.

The Message in Brief

Paul feels deeply for his Jewish brothers and sisters. He is saddened because they were chosen out of all the people of the world to be God's children, and yet, they have forsaken the Lord by rejecting Jesus as their Savior. But it pleases Paul that the Gentiles have received and embraced God's promises. Even though they are not genetically descended from Abraham, the Gentiles have received those promises from God first given to Abraham. God has chosen believers, regardless of national or ethnic backgrounds, to be His children. We praise God for choosing us through faith in Jesus to be His children. He has given salvation to His chosen believers in Christ not by anything we have done, but purely out of His love and compassion for us.

Working with the Text

The Blessings of God's Choice (Romans 9:1–9)

1. Do you remember how in chapter 3 Paul mentioned the advantages of being a Jew? Here in chapter 9 Paul returns to the theme. Paul mentioned in Romans 3:2 how the people of Israel were first entrusted with God's Word. Out of all the people of the world, the Jews were the first to receive His Holy Word. Read Romans 9:4–5 and list the other blessings given to the Jews as God's chosen people.

2. Paul himself was of Jewish ancestry. He felt a bond and kinship with his Jewish brothers and sisters. How does Paul describe his feelings toward the Jews who had rejected Jesus as their Messiah and Savior from sin (vv. 2–3)? How does his feeling compare to Christ's feeling for the people of the world as He sacrificed Himself on the cross?

3. The good news is that God's promises through Jesus Christ are no longer only for the Jews. Those promises are received by all who trust in Him. Unfortunately, many of the Jews in Paul's day had abandoned the

Lord by rejecting Jesus. As Paul states in verses 6–7: "For not all who are descended from Israel are Israel. Nor because they are his descendants are they all Abraham's children."

Now a little background information. God promised Abraham (the father of the Jews) and Sarah (his wife) they would have children, but they grew very old without seeing the promise fulfilled. In desperation, Sarah used her handmaiden, Hagar, to bear Abraham's child. But this was not the child that God had promised. So even though Hagar's child, Ishmael, was a natural child of Abraham, he was not the child of the promise (see v. 8). When Abraham was 100 years old, he was finally blessed with Isaac, the son whom God had promised. So, what's Paul's point here? Natural descent does not make one an heir to God's promises (as the Jews believed). Otherwise, Ishmael would have been the child of promise. Those who believe God's promise of eternal life through Jesus are the true "children of the promise," whether Jew or Gentile. Discuss as a group your various ethnic backgrounds. From what country did most of your ancestors come? How many different countries are represented in the group?

The Mystery of God's Choice (Romans 9:10–21)

1. Some more background information: Paul describes Abraham's son Isaac as the child of the promise. Isaac married a woman named Rebekah. She and Isaac had twins who were named Jacob and Esau. Of the two twins, Esau was born first. Technically, he should have been the heir to the Lord's promises through his father Isaac. But it would not work out that way. Jacob would receive the promise instead. Through Jacob's descendants God would create a special people. As a matter of fact, Jacob's name would be changed to Israel. That is why the Jews were commonly called the "people of Israel." Even though Esau deserved the promise, Jacob received it. In many ways, this doesn't seem fair. Read Malachi 1:2–3 and explain how the Lord "elected" Jacob over Esau. How is this a good example of God's election of certain people to be His? How does the Lord describe the process of election in Romans 9:15 and Exodus 33:19?

"I have loved you," says the LORD. "But you ask, 'How have You loved us?'

"Was not Esau Jacob's brother?" the LORD says. "Yet I have loved Jacob, but Esau I have hated, and I have turned his mountains into a wasteland and left his inheritance to the desert jackals." Malachi 1:2–3

For He says to Moses, "I will have mercy on whom I have mercy, and I will have compassion on whom I have compassion." Romans 9:15

And the LORD said, "I will cause all My goodness to pass in front of you, and I will proclaim My name, the LORD, in your presence. I will have mercy on whom I will have mercy, and I will have compassion on whom I will have compassion." Exodus 33:19

2. If it is true that God will have mercy on whom He chooses (v. 18), what does this mean about our attempts to earn His forgiveness and salvation? Is merit the basis on which He chooses people? What does Paul say about this in verse 16?

3. A natural response to election is to question why God would judge those whose hearts He Himself has hardened. Paul gives no firm answer to this puzzling question. Rather, he uses an illustration of why it is not in our power to question God. Describe his illustration (v. 21) in your own words.

4. An interesting biblical example of hearts being hardened can be found in Mark 3:20–30. Who do some of the teachers of the law accuse Jesus of being? Their denial of Jesus as the Son of God is considered

blaspheming the Holy Spirit. Knowing that the Holy Spirit brings people to faith in Jesus, why would blaspheming the Spirit cause a hardening of the heart? Turn to Mark 4:9–12 and notice how when people reject the Holy Spirit they no longer understand the things of the Spirit—including God's Word.

> Then Jesus said, "He who has ears to hear, let him hear."
>
> When He was alone, the Twelve and the others around Him asked Him about the parables. He told them, "The secret of the kingdom of God has been given to you. But to those on the outside everything is said in parables so that, 'they may be ever seeing but never perceiving, and ever hearing but never understanding; otherwise they might turn and be forgiven!'" Mark 4:9–12

The Mercy in God's Choice (Romans 9:22–33)

1. God is merciful. In His mercy, He even shows patience toward "the objects of His wrath" (Romans 9:22). According to Romans 2:4, what is the reason for His patience toward unbelievers? How is this supported in 2 Peter 3:9?

> The Lord is not slow in keeping His promise, as some understand slowness. He is patient with you, not wanting anyone to perish, but everyone to come to repentance. 2 Peter 3:9

2. Many of the Jews have not understood or have rejected God's plan of righteousness through Jesus Christ. Notice the quotation from Isaiah that is found in Romans 9:33. *Zion* is another name for Jerusalem, and is often used symbolically to refer to the Jews. Who is the stumbling block for Zion? Although this stumbling block impedes deliverance for some, who receives the gift of redemption through it?

3. In what way do the Gentile Christians pursue righteousness according to Romans 9:30? But how do the unbelieving Jews pursue righteousness? Who is most successful in finding true righteousness in God's eyes?

Applying the Message

1. The Bible's description of election is important to understand. Although some people are chosen for salvation in Jesus Christ, *the rest are not chosen for damnation.* This doesn't make logical sense, but it is the way in which God's Word portrays God's election. A similar mystery surrounds the manner in which people receive the Lord. The Bible teaches that people cannot decide on their own to believe in Jesus as their Savior and Lord. And yet people have the power to reject Jesus. There is no logical resolution to this paradox. In these areas, faith must transcend reason. Read 1 Corinthians 1:18; 2:14; and 12:3 and Matthew 23:37. How do these verses support the contention that we have the power to reject the Lord but not to accept the Lord?

For the message of the cross is foolishness to those who are perishing, but to us who are being saved it is the power of God. 1 Corinthians 1:18

The man without the Spirit does not accept the things that come from the Spirit of God, for they are foolishness to him, and he cannot understand them, because they are spiritually discerned. 1 Corinthians 2:14

Therefore I tell you that no one who is speaking by the Spirit of God says, "Jesus be cursed," and no one can say, "Jesus is Lord," except by the Holy Spirit. 1 Corinthians 12:3

O Jerusalem, Jerusalem, you who kill the prophets and stone those sent to you, how often I have longed to gather your children together, as a hen gathers her chicks under her wings, but you were not willing. Matthew 23:37

2. In Romans 9:27, Paul quotes a passage from Isaiah that predicts only a remnant of the people of Israel will be saved. Indeed, today there are some Jews who have received the gift of faith in Christ Jesus. In a very literal way, they could be considered "the remnant of Israel." Are you aware of the names of some of the organizations that are made up of Jewish Christians in ministry to their Lord? What do you think it would feel like to be raised with great hopes about the coming Messiah, only to discover He has already come?

3. Unbelieving Jews are not the only ones on this planet who are pursuing righteousness (goodness) in God's eyes by their accomplishments. List some other examples of people who feel they are accepted in their god's eyes by what they do.

Taking the Message Home

Review

Imagine, if you can, what the world would be like if some people were considered predestined to eternal life while others were predestined to eternal damnation. How would the two groups be determined? What would it feel like to be damned for eternity? God does not predetermine some to damnation. He wants all people to be saved. Some are predestined to salvation, but the rest are not predestined to damnation.

Although this may not seem logical, what comfort does it bring to believers? How does it inspire believers to continue to share the good news of salvation through Jesus Christ with unbelievers?

Looking Ahead

When time permits, read Romans 10. What important understandings did you gain from this reading? Write down the points you found most interesting and be ready to share them with others at the beginning of the next session.

Working Ahead

Complete one or more of the following suggestions before the next session:

1. Ask the pastor of your church what he enjoys most about preaching and teaching God's Word. Although there are many other tasks that occupy a pastor's time, his preaching and teaching are most visible. What does your pastor hope will happen as a result of his preaching and teaching?

2. Reflect on this question: Is it possible to believe and trust in the Lord Jesus without ever stating so? Why or why not?

3. On the other hand, if someone simply says, "I believe in Jesus," without knowing who Jesus really is or what He accomplished, do you think that person has salvation? Why or why not?

Did You Know . . .

Many of the quotations Paul uses in his writings come from the prophet Isaiah. Isaiah was born around 765 B.C. The Lord mightily used the prophet not only to predict the future captivity of God's people by the Babylonians, but also to foresee the restoration of Israel. Many of Isaiah's prophecies also pointed to the coming of Jesus Christ. Perhaps the clearest picture of Jesus' ministry is described in Isaiah 53. There is no one in history who has fulfilled this description except for Jesus. And many of Isaiah's prophecies underscored the future incorporation of all the peoples of the world into God's kingdom, whether Jew or Gentile, through faith in the Messiah, Jesus. Today, as we watch the Christian church grow throughout the world, we continue to see the fulfillment of the prophecies spoken by Isaiah more than 700 years before the birth of Christ.

Biblical Examples of
Hardened Hearts

Exodus 8:15—But when Pharaoh saw that there was relief, he hardened his heart and would not listen to Moses and Aaron, just as the LORD had said.

2 Chronicles 36:13—He (King Zedekiah) also rebelled against King Nebuchadnezzar, who had made him take an oath in God's name. He became stiff-necked and hardened his heart and would not turn to the LORD, the God of Israel.

Psalm 78:32—In spite of all this, they (the people of Israel) kept on sinning; in spite of His (God's) wonders, they did not believe.

Jeremiah 5:3—You struck them (the people of Israel), but they felt no pain; You crushed them, but they refused correction. They made their faces harder than stone and refused to repent.

Daniel 5:20—But when his (King Nebuchadnezzar's) heart became arrogant and hardened with pride, he was deposed from his royal throne and stripped of his glory.

Zechariah 7:11-12—But they (the people of Israel) refused to pay attention; stubbornly they turned their backs and stopped up their ears. They made their hearts as hard as flint and would not listen to the law or to the words that the LORD Almighty had sent by His Spirit through the earlier prophets.

Session 8

The Righteous Remnant

(Romans 10:1–11:24)

Approaching This Study

Christians find it difficult to endure unbelief in Jesus expressed by those they love. Some Christian fathers and mothers feel despair as they watch their children grow to reject the Lord. Brothers and sisters may question why their siblings cannot enjoy their same deep relationship with the Lord. And believers may find it difficult to comprehend the hostility toward God and His church demonstrated by friends and loved ones. This is nothing new. Paul felt great sorrow toward his Jewish brothers and sisters who rejected Jesus as the long-awaited Messiah. Even as Paul grieved, however, he recognized their unbelief as something foreseen in Scripture. The prophets of the Old Testament had frequently referred to a "remnant" of God's people, who would be delivered. The concept of the remnant implies that others would reject God's plan of salvation through faith in Jesus. In this session, Paul comes to terms with the sad reality of those who turn away from God's promises. But Paul turns with a hopeful heart to the many Gentiles who will hear and receive the promises of forgiveness and eternal life through Jesus Christ. It is a wonderful gift to be chosen by God. And, demonstrating his genuine and authentic love for others, Paul can only feel sadness for those who reject this indescribable gift.

An Overview

Unit Reading

Read Romans 10:1–11:24.

The Message in Brief

Once again Paul expresses his desire for the Jews to turn to Jesus and receive salvation. But he appreciates the opportunity to bring the message of salvation to the Gentiles. The Gentiles, too, will know the blessings of being chosen by God for salvation. Both Jew and Gentile will only hear the message as a result of those who are sent to preach the Gospel of God's grace and forgiveness.

Joyfully, Paul recognizes that not all the Jews will reject their Savior. A remnant of Israelites will continue to uphold and trust the promises of God in His Son. Even though the Israelites are like a branch that has been torn from the trunk of God's tree, that branch may one day be grafted back onto the tree. That is Paul's ongoing hope.

Working with the Text

The Righteousness That Is by Faith (Romans 10:1–13)

1. How does Paul define the relationship between the Israelites (the Jews) and God? How do the Jews feel about God? Why is their zealous relationship insufficient for salvation, according to verses 2–4? Now, consider the popular idea that those who have a sincere belief in any god will be saved. How would Paul respond?

2. We are granted forgiveness and eternal life simply by trusting they are ours in Jesus Christ. But this is too simple for many people. What illustrations does Paul use to show that we cannot by our own endeavors gain salvation (vv. 6–7)?

3. Evidence of genuine faith is found in both the heart and the mouth. What must the heart believe to receive salvation (v. 9)? What confession flows from the mouth of one who believes in Jesus?

No Excuse for Israel (Romans 10:14–21)

1. Verses 14 and 15 define—in a reverse fashion—the process by which the Word of God enters the hearts of God's people. What happens when one believes in the Lord? But what must happen before one can believe? And who must be available to cause people to hear? And how are these people made available? So, what value does Paul place on those who preach God's Word?

2. What must happen before faith comes to a person, according to verse 17? As a result of this and other passages, Christians call the Word of God a "means of grace." Think about that phrase. Based on what Paul says in this verse, how is this an appropriate expression?

3. In verses 19 and 20, Paul quotes Deuteronomy 32:21 and Isaiah 65:1. How do both of these passages underscore God's determination to give His message of salvation to the Gentiles once it has been rejected by the Jews?

The Remnant (Romans 11:1–10)

1. As Paul considers the fate of the Jews, he contemplates whether God has abandoned His chosen people, the Israelites. Has He? Who rejected who?

2. Read the story of Elijah and his flight from wicked King Ahab and Queen Jezebel in 1 Kings 19:1–18. What feeling did Elijah have after being threatened by the king and queen?

But what did God promise in 1 Kings 19:18? Now turn back to Romans 11:2–4. How does Paul use Elijah's story to illustrate the wonderful truth that not all of Israel will reject Jesus? What does Paul call this select group of believers in verse 5?

3. What happened to those Jews who were not part of the elect? How was God involved in this process?

The Gentiles Grafted onto the Tree of Life (Romans 11:11–24)

1. The rejection of Jesus by the Jews was not all bad. What wonderful consequence did it have? What consequence for the Jews does Paul hope will emerge as a result of God providing His promise of salvation to the Gentiles?

2. Paul compares the Gentile Christians to a wild olive shoot that is grafted onto an existing olive tree. The shoot is grafted onto the plant only after other olive branches—representing the Jews—are broken off. What caused the olive branches to be broken off? What caused the shoot to be grafted on? Should this be a source of arrogance for the Gentile Christians? Why or why not?

3. Is it possible for the severed olive branches to be grafted back onto the tree? How does this answer relate to Paul's description of the remnant of Israel?

Applying the Message

1. We may sometimes question why faith in Jesus' death and resurrection is so important for salvation. It might be tempting to question why God doesn't just save everyone. The fact is, God *has* saved everyone! But there are many who reject the salvation Jesus won for them on the cross. Let's use this analogy. Suppose you won a national sweepstakes. Your prize is one million dollars. A representative of the sweepstakes company arrives at your door to deliver the gift in the form of a check. A check, after all, is a simple promise the money will be transferred to your account. When you open the door and receive the check, you refuse to believe the check is valid. Can you think of some reasons a person might question the authenticity of such a check? If the winner of the sweepstakes is so skeptical that he or she refuses to cash the check, would that person receive the winnings? Now, replace the representative of the sweepstakes company with Jesus Christ. He comes to our door and offers us the gift of eternal life in the promise of His Word. Why do you think some people refuse to "cash in on" the promise? Whose fault is it if the recipient of the check is too skeptical to cash it?

2. Paul was deeply disturbed by the reluctance of his own people to trust in the gift won for them through Jesus' death and resurrection. As a result of the Jews' unbelief, Paul says, God turned and offered the promise of salvation to the Gentiles. When one group of people rejects the Lord, He will turn to another. How do you see this process working in our world today? Ask your pastor about the growth of Christian

churches in Europe and North America compared to the growth occurring among Christian churches in Africa, Central and South America, and Asia.

3. "Faith comes from hearing the message, and the message is heard through the word of Christ." With these words, Paul indicates the importance of those who publicly proclaim the Gospel message. Through the words of the preacher, Christ is heard. And when Christ is heard, the Holy Spirit works faith in the hearts of unbelievers and strengthens the faith of believers. If preaching is so important to God's church, how do you think the devil views it? What can people who proclaim God's Word expect from Satan? Why, then, do you think the pastoral office is much more difficult than just leading the worship services on Sunday morning?

Taking the Message Home

Review

Read Romans 10:11–13. Reflect on the blessings you receive through membership in God's church through saving faith in Jesus Christ.

Looking Ahead

If time permits, read Romans 11:25–12:21. God's grace and love to us as His chosen people cause us to think and behave differently toward others. Make a list of the ways in which Christian sisters and brothers treat each other as a result of their chosen status.

Working Ahead

Complete one or more of the following suggestions before the next session:

1. Ponder some examples of God's mysterious ways. Think of experi-

ences from your life when God resolved a problem or issue in the most unexpected way. Be prepared to share this experience during the next session.

2. In what ways do you think our lives and bodies should be given to the Lord as "living sacrifices"? How should we treat the gift of our bodies and lives? How can they be used to give God glory?

3. By now, you have probably become acquainted with a number of the participants in your group. You may have noticed some special talents or abilities possessed by some of them. On a piece of paper, list those individuals and their special abilities.

Did You Know . . .

"Remnant" is an ongoing theme in Scripture. When the world was destroyed in the great flood, Noah and his family were the remnant delivered from death to replenish the earth. When Israel was taken into exile by the Assyrians and Babylonians, a remnant of them returned to restore Jerusalem and its temple. And with the coming of Jesus Christ, only a remnant of the Jews would believe in Him and be saved. In a way, today's Christian church stands as a remnant, elected by God from among the world's population to receive faith in the promises of forgiveness and eternal life. What does it feel like to know you are part of the remnant?

Session 9

Responding to Our Election

(Romans 11:25–12:21)

Approaching This Study

Let's face it. God's election is completely mysterious. Really, there is no reason why He has chosen you or me for eternal life. But when we believe in Jesus as our Savior, there is a guarantee that we have been chosen. We are part of the elect. We have no reason to spend sleepless nights questioning God's wisdom and insight in choosing us or others. Our response is not endless questioning and investigation. Instead we respond in praise and thanksgiving, as we strive to follow God's will. God has given us so much, we joyfully lift our hearts and hands to serve Him.

God has even given us the tools to serve Him. His Spirit has given us gifts that we are to use to build each other up, to uplift His church, and to work for the growth of His kingdom. And by the power of the Spirit, God gives us the ability to love one another, not in the way perceived by so many in our society, but with the commitment to sacrifice a part of ourselves for others. As we read this next session of Romans, we thank the Lord for His mercy, we bask in the grace and love of our majestic and mysterious God, and we ask God for opportunities to serve Him so that His love will be revealed to others.

An Overview

Unit Reading

Read Romans 11:25–12:21.

The Message in Brief

The people of Israel, chosen by God as His special nation, rejected Jesus as their Lord and Savior. As a result, God turned to the Gentiles and offered them the gift of eternal life through Jesus' death. Paul is saddened by the hardened hearts displayed by the Jews, but he recognizes that their unbelief opens the door for salvation to be received by the Gentiles. Paul will not completely discard his sisters and brothers in Judaism. He knows they were chosen by God, and although they may have rejected the Lord, the Lord will never reject them. All those who turn to Jesus as their Savior will be saved. And so, Paul praises God for His mysterious election. As a result of our election, Paul implores us to respond in a God-pleasing fashion by using the gifts God has given us to uplift others and to show love for our brothers and sisters in Christ. Christian love is different than the perception of love commonly held by society. It involves sacrifice and commitment. It reflects the love of Christ, which was graphically demonstrated when He gave His very life on the cross for our eternal salvation.

Working with the Text

The Salvation of Israel (Romans 11:25–36)

1. The Gentile Christians might have been tempted to believe they were superior to the Jews because God had chosen them to receive Jesus Christ after the Jews had rejected Him. But God patiently waits for the Israelites to receive His mercy. In the meantime, what will God accomplish among the Gentiles?

2. There are many Christians who look at Romans 11:26 and interpret Paul's words "all Israel will be saved" as a promise the Lord will eventually save all the Jews, perhaps giving them a "second chance" to confess Jesus as their Lord after they have died. But there is no indication in Scripture that any sort of second chance exists for anyone after death. And unfortunately, Romans 11:14 expresses Paul's hope that at least *some* of the Jews will turn to Jesus and be saved, implying that many Jews will *not* be saved. So the comment "all Israel will be saved" cannot stand as a promise of salvation for all Jews. Other Christians view Romans 11:26 as a prophecy about the Last Days, when they believe the nation of Israel will be converted into a Christian state. Of course, God could accomplish this miracle. But a more likely interpretation is based on Paul's previous comment that a time will arrive when the "full num-

ber of the Gentiles" will be saved. By this expression he did not mean that *all* Gentiles will be saved, but rather that the complete number ordained by God will be saved. In the same way, when Paul refers to "all Israel" being saved, he is referring to the complete number of Jews throughout the generations that make up the remnant elected by God. Paul may also be referring to the total number of the elect, both Jews and Gentiles, who constitute the "spiritual" descendants of Abraham— a sort of "spiritual" Israel.

Because the Gentiles receive Jesus while the Jews reject Him, how do the Jews feel about the Gentiles, according to Romans 11:28? But what is God's feeling toward the Jews? Why (vv. 28–29)?

3. How does the doxology of Romans 11:33–36 define the unique wisdom and knowledge of God?

Using Our Gifts (Romans 12:1–8)

1. In response to the mystery and majesty of our election to salvation through Jesus Christ, we respond in thanksgiving. We give our very lives to the Lord, or, as Paul puts it, we "offer [our] bodies as living sacrifices." God's grace motivates us to reject conformity to the evil around us. Instead, we are transformed by the power of the Holy Spirit working through God's Word to follow His will and His ways. To help us in this endeavor God has given all believers various gifts. What gifts does Paul list in Romans 12:6–8?

2. What other gifts are mentioned in Scripture? See 1 Corinthians 12:7–11, 27–30 and Ephesians 4:11–13.

3. What are the purposes of these gifts, and who determines which gifts are given to whom? See Romans 12:4–5; 1 Corinthians 12:11–26; and Ephesians 4:7, 12–13.

Loving One Another (Romans 12:9–21)

1. Romans 12:9–19 includes a number of exhortations for Christian living. Summarize this section in your own words, in your own mind, or on paper; then share your summary with the group.

2. As we show love to one another, Paul entreats us to "be willing to associate with people of low position." How is this admonition contrary to the philosophy held by most people? Share with one another examples of people you have known or heard about who have worked and cared for "people of low position."

3. Followers of Christ are urged to abstain from acts of revenge. Who will perform that function for us (Romans 12:19)? If we believe the Lord is in charge of fulfilling justice and avenging offenses, what are we free to do (Romans 12:20)?

4. Paul exhorts us to "hate what is evil; cling to what is good." If Christians take this to heart, what difference will result in their lifestyles? How will it affect the movies they watch, the books they read, and their activities, hobbies, and habits? How does Christianity pull people away from conformity to the world?

Applying the Message

1. After reflecting on the spiritual gifts that Paul listed, which do you think you possess? How do you know that these are your spiritual gifts? What gifts do others in your group display?

2. Many of Paul's exhortations for Christian living involve caring for and working with one another. We are to honor others above ourselves, practice hospitality, bless those who persecute us, live in harmony with one another, and live at peace with everyone. But, within many congregations, divisions and confrontations frequently arise over rather trivial issues. Read James 4:1–3. What causes these quarrels? What does the Bible say about those who are divisive and contentious (Titus 3:10)?

What causes fights and quarrels among you? Don't they come from your desires that battle within you? You want something but don't get it. You kill and covet, but you cannot have what you want. You quarrel and fight. You do not have, because you do not ask God. When you ask, you do not receive, because you ask with wrong motives, that you may spend what you get on your pleasures. James 4:1–3

Warn a divisive person once, and then warn him a second time. After that, have nothing to do with him. Titus 3:10

3. Paul concludes Romans 12 with this powerful exhortation: "Do not be overcome by evil, but overcome evil with good." Is this really possible? Can people defeat the forces of evil around them by loving others in response to God's love in Christ? Share your opinions and examples with one another.

Taking the Message Home

Review

Spend some time meditating on the various ways you are determined to not "conform any longer to the pattern of this world, but be transformed by the renewing of your mind." List three spiritual goals for the upcoming year. What are three ways in which you would like to grow closer to the Lord this year? Remember, the Holy Spirit strengthens our faith as we spend time in God's Word.

Looking Ahead

Read Romans 13 before the next session. How would your life change if you knew the Lord would return before the month was over? How would you change your priorities and perspectives?

Working Ahead

Complete one or more of the following suggestions before the next session:

1. Be prepared to share your opinion about dissent against the government. When should a Christian disobey the authority and law of government? Should the Christian view government as a necessary evil or as a blessing from God?

2. Some organizations that call themselves "Christian militia" insist they will no longer pay taxes because they feel the government has no right to tax them. Do you think taxation is necessary? What would you do to change the present tax system?

3. Read the Ten Commandments as recorded in Exodus 20:1–17. Do

you consider the Ten Commandments a yoke by which we are constrained to follow a certain lifestyle, or do you think they are a gracious guide to a fulfilling and contented life? In what ways could these commandments be considered a guide for loving God and our fellow humans?

Did You Know . . .

Love is a common theme in the Bible. Again and again we are called upon to love each other. People often misunderstand the definition of biblical love because the word *love* is used in so many ways today, incorporating a number of definitions. Paul defines love in 1 Corinthians 13:4–8: "Love is patient, love is kind. It does not envy, it does not boast, it is not proud. It is not rude, it is not self-seeking, it is not easily angered, it keeps no record of wrongs. Love does not delight in evil but rejoices with the truth. It always protects, always trusts, always hopes, always perseveres. Love never fails." Biblical love is sometimes called *agape*, after the Greek word for "selfless love." Unlike the erotic love frequently portrayed by television and the movies, agape love is sacrificial and intentional. Biblical love involves a commitment, a determination, an intention to care for someone despite his or her undeserving nature. Jesus demonstrated agape love as He died on the cross for our sins. A husband and wife commit to agape love in their marriage vows. They strive to intentionally love each other even when the erotic love wanes and the "feeling" of love lessens. If all people understood the meaning of *agape* and reflected it in their daily lives, the world would be transformed.

Spiritual Gifts Listed in Scripture

Special People Gifts:
Apostle
Prophet
Evangelist
Pastor-Teacher
Teacher

Speaking Gifts:
Exhortation
Wisdom
Knowledge

Serving Gifts:
Serving
Helping
Leadership
Administration
Giving
Showing Mercy
Discernment
Faith
Hospitality

Sign Gifts:
Tongues
Interpretation
Miracles
Healing

From Dean W. Nadasdy, *Concerning Spiritual Gifts*, p. 26. © 1994 CPH. Used by permission.

Session 10

The Response Continues

(Romans 13)

Approaching This Study

What is the Christian's obligation toward government? As Paul continues his discussion about the believer's response to God's grace demonstrated in the person and work of Jesus Christ, he introduces the duties of the Christian to the state. The Christian church has often struggled with the governments alongside of which it has operated. In fact, Christianity was born in turmoil during the rule of the Roman government, which engaged in several serious persecutions of God's people. Only after Constantine became emperor of the Roman Empire in A.D. 312 did Christianity become the religion of the state. And as difficult as it may have been for the church to thrive under a hostile government, it was even more impossible for the church to maintain its Gospel-oriented purpose when church and state were merged!

Paul encourages Christians to support and honor their government. There is no biblical mandate for the kind of government that should be supported. Paul simply states that all who have been placed in authority have received their positions from God. Thus, they should be honored as God's representative in the world to maintain law and order. The Christian has a duty to support the government by paying taxes and respecting the offices of the government.

But the Christian is to support and respect not only the government; the Christian's response to God's grace also motivates a respect toward others. We demonstrate Christian love for each other by following God's Law found in the Ten Commandments. When we do so, we protect and uplift our neighbors. Words and actions that are constructive, positive, and edifying to others are expressions of Christian love.

We dedicate ourselves to the response that comes from faith in Jesus Christ. We have no idea when our earthly lives will come to an end and we will meet our Savior face-to-face. Neither do we know when Christ will come again to judge the world. We live as if that moment is imminent, spending our time in service and devotion to our Lord. Time is wasting! Let's serve the Lord!

An Overview

Unit Reading

Divide the reading from Romans 13 into the following sections: 13:1–5, 6–7, 8–10, and 11–14.

The Message in Brief

God in His grace and mercy elected believers in Christ into eternity. Paul continues his discussion of our response to this incredible election by encouraging Christians to obey those whom God has placed in authority. Specifically, Paul focuses on government authorities who maintain order and enforce the law. Paul reminds his readers that God has placed those who govern into their position. When we obey the government, we demonstrate obedience to our Lord and we keep ourselves safe from criminal punishment. Paul tells us to not only respect and honor the officials of the state, but also to pay our taxes.

The Christian demonstrates love for God and others by following the Ten Commandments. These commandments outline behaviors that bring no injury to others and honor God. As we await the return of our Lord Jesus, Paul encourages us to follow God's Law. With each new day, we are brought closer to the moment when we will be with Jesus, either as a result of His return or our earthly death. We spend our remaining time abstaining from immoral living while serving and obeying our Lord Jesus Christ.

Working with the Text

Submitting to Authority (Romans 13:1–7)

1. According to Romans 13:1–5, how are we to view our leaders in government? Why? According to Paul, how does one avoid living in fear from the government?

2. Does God mandate we follow the laws of our government no matter what? This has been a source of controversy throughout the history of the church. For example, many Lutherans wrestled with the question of their submission to Hitler's regime. Perhaps one of the most famous martyrs of that time was Dietrich Bonhoeffer, a Lutheran pastor and professor, whose opposition to fascism resulted in imprisonment and execution. What is the Christian to do when a government establishes laws that clearly violate God's will? Peter and the other apostles faced this problem when confronted by the Sanhedrin, the ruling Jewish religious officials in Jerusalem. The Sanhedrin commanded the apostles to refrain from preaching the Gospel of Jesus Christ. Of course, this was in direct violation to Christ's mandate. Read Matthew 28:18–20. What was the last command Jesus gave His disciples? So, how did Peter and the apostles respond to the Sanhedrin's demand that they silence themselves (Acts 5:29)? If time permits look up Daniel 3:1–18. Describe Shadrach, Meshach, and Abednego's response to an ungodly law. How does their response provide a "rule of thumb" for Christians who are burdened with immoral governmental laws?

Then Jesus came to them and said, "All authority in heaven and on earth has been given to Me. Therefore go and make disciples of all nations, baptizing them in the name of the Father and of the Son and of the Holy Spirit, and teaching them to obey everything I have commanded you. And surely I am with you always, to the very end of the age. Matthew 28:18–20

Peter and the other apostles replied: "We must obey God rather than men!" Acts 5:29

3. How is the Christian to respond to taxes? Is it legitimate to cheat the government? Look up what Jesus had to say about this issue in Matthew 22:15–22. How does Paul echo Jesus' advice?

Love Means Following the Commandments (Romans 13:8–10)

1. Movies and television attempt to depict love in a fashion that often contradicts the love described in Scripture. According to Paul, what do we follow in order to show our love for one another? Why?

2. Why is obedience to the commandment "Do not commit adultery" the only genuine way to express love even if two people not married to each other are strongly attracted to one another?

3. Look up *covet* in a dictionary and write down its meaning. How do we show love for each other when we do not covet?

The Hour Is Near (Romans 13:11–14)

1. In what way is your salvation nearer now than when you first believed in Jesus Christ?

2. How does Paul describe our existence in this fallen world as we await the return of our Lord (v. 12)? What behaviors are we called upon to avoid as we wait?

3. How do you understand the exhortation to "clothe yourselves with the Lord Jesus Christ"? According to Galatians 3:26–27, when did that "clothing" begin? How does Ephesians 4:22–24 help explain what Paul asks of us when we are called upon to "clothe" ourselves in Jesus Christ? How does Colossians 3:12–14 assist your understanding?

You are all sons of God through faith in Christ Jesus, for all of you who were baptized into Christ have clothed yourselves with Christ. Galatians 3:26–27

You were taught, with regard to your former way of life, to put off your old self, which is being corrupted by its deceitful desires; to be made new in the attitude of your minds; and to put on the new self, created to be like God in true righteousness and holiness. Ephesians 4:22–24

Therefore, as God's chosen people, holy and dearly loved, clothe yourselves with compassion, kindness, humility, gentleness and patience. Bear with each other and forgive whatever grievances you may have against one another. Forgive as the Lord forgave you. And over all these virtues put on love, which binds them all together in perfect unity. Colossians 3:12–14

Applying the Message

1. It seems impossible for Christians to completely avoid conflict with the laws of government. When the government commands an action contrary to God's will, the Christian must disobey the government. How might the Christian respond to a government that requires the following:

(a) Only two children are allowed per family; any other pregnancies must be aborted.

(b) Christians may not worship together upon threat of imprisonment.

(c) African Americans cannot eat in the same restaurant as Caucasians.

(d) The military must invade a nation for the sole purpose of seizing and acquiring its natural resources.

2. Does the Bible tell us when Jesus will return? Look up Matthew 24:36. Who knows the day of Jesus' return? What does this suggest about those who prophesy the date of Jesus' return? Even though we may not see the Lord's return in our lifetime, why do we prepare to meet the Lord at any moment (Luke 23:39–43)? Knowing you may see the Lord at any time—even if it is because of sudden death—how will you resolve to live a life reflecting God's will?

Taking the Message Home

Review

As time permits, read Romans 13 again. In what way do you think this chapter could change your attitude about the political offices of government? Will you be reminded of this chapter during the next tax season? How has your perspective on the Ten Commandments changed?

Looking Ahead

Read Romans 14 before the next session. Reflect on an incident in which someone claiming to be a Christian publicly demonstrated offensive behavior. What happened? How did it reflect on the Christian church? How can immoral or offensive behavior by Christians obstruct the work of the Holy Spirit in bringing people to faith?

Working Ahead

Complete one or more of the following suggestions before the next session:

1. If you know someone who is a vegetarian, ask that person to help you answer these questions before the next session. Why do some people avoid meat altogether? What benefits may the strict vegetarian receive? What dangers may exist if one abstains from meat?

2. What is your favorite holiday? Research the major religious holidays of Judaism. You might do this by looking in an encyclopedia, browsing the Internet, or talking with a Jewish friend. Which is their most important holiday? What other holy days do they observe?

3. Reflect on the various foods and drinks available today. Are there any foods or beverages you would consider evil or sinful? Why? Are they evil in and of themselves, or are they used by some people for sinful purposes?

Did You Know . . .

Dietrich Bonhoeffer (1906–1945) was a child of a famous neurologist in Germany. As he grew up, Bonhoeffer became more interested in theology and philosophy than in medicine. In time, he was ordained as a Lutheran pastor, ministering to German congregations in Barcelona and London. As he grew more concerned about the nazification of the German church under Adolph Hitler, he emerged as the leader of the German Confessing Church, opposing the Nazi-supported church government, which functioned under the leadership of Ludwig Miller. The tenacity of the Confessing Church helped discredit Miller's leadership because its existence demonstrated that the Lutheran church was not uniformly submissive to the Nazi regime. And its witness to Christ's supreme reign over the world challenged Hitler's claims of totalitarianism. Bonhoeffer founded a seminary for training pastors, but the seminary was short-lived. His license to teach was revoked in 1936, and Heinrich Himmler, the Nazi Reichsführer SS, closed the seminary in 1937. Bonhoeffer then spent much time traveling, hoping to inspire concern for the predicament of the Lutheran church in Germany. He became involved in the Resistance movement, and this led to his arrest by the Gestapo in 1943. He was hanged on a charge of treason on April 9, 1945, in a concentration camp at Flossenbürg. There now exists a simple tablet in Flossenbürg's village church with the inscription "Dietrich Bonhoeffer, a witness of Jesus Christ among his brethren."

Although Paul exhorts followers of Christ to submit to the government, Bonhoeffer is a shining example of the principle that "we must obey God rather than men" (Acts 5:29).

Session 11

Giving Up Our "Rights" for Others

(Romans 14)

Approaching This Study

Not only is self-centeredness one result of our original sin, it is also fashionable in today's culture. We live in a society that stresses individual rights over the needs and concerns of others. In contrast to our prevailing culture, the call of Christ involves service to each other. One of the basic consequences of receiving the overwhelming love of God in Jesus Christ is the desire to reflect His love by showing care and compassion for others. This basic tenet is highlighted in Romans 14. Paul highlights the need to set aside our Christian rights in deference to those who may be offended by our actions and lose respect for the Gospel of Jesus Christ.

The setting for this discussion arises from the conflict between the Jewish and Gentile Christians in Rome. Whereas the Gentile Christians were much more comfortable living under the freedom of the Gospel, the Jewish Christians were influenced by their Old Testament roots. The Jewish Christians viewed some foods as unclean and immoral. Because of their background, they had difficulty accepting the concept that all food was clean. Paul uses this issue to underscore the liberty of the Gospel. God calls on Christians to obey the moral Law, but the ceremonial and dietary laws of the Old Testament are no longer necessary. These laws pointed to the coming of the Messiah, but since Jesus has already lived, died, risen, and ascended, they are no longer relevant. Look up Colossians 2:16–17 and reflect on what Paul writes about such restrictions. With what words does he indicate their obsolescence?

Although most Christians are not arguing about dietary laws today, the principle Paul expresses remains applicable in many areas. We are called to abstain from behavior that may not be immoral but might offend those not quite as strong in their faith. Out of consideration and care for others, we restrict what we do and say. Our goal is the salvation of souls. We avoid those things that may hinder another's faith in the Lord.

An Overview

Unit Reading

One volunteer can read this entire chapter. Then reread Romans 14:19–20, as it is the focus of this chapter's exhortation.

The Message in Brief

Paul's discussion about our response to God's election and grace continues in this chapter. He focuses on those who possess a weaker faith and feel compelled to follow certain laws from which they have already been freed. They may not yet fully accept their freedom and may feel offended by those who flaunt such freedom. Out of care and consideration for the souls of such brothers and sisters in Christ, mature Christians will refrain from parading their freedoms. The weaker Christian must not be repelled from the faith by behavior she or he might consider offensive. As we continue together on our journeys of faith, Christians constantly seek unity, peace, and mutual edification.

Working with the Text

To Eat or Not to Eat (Romans 14:1–8)

1. As Paul explores the freedom of living under the grace and forgiveness of Jesus Christ, he raises the issue of dietary laws. How does he describe the faith of those who feel they should only eat vegetables? Today, many people are vegetarians for health reasons rather than spiritual reasons. But Paul is expressing the principle that no food in and of itself is evil. For that matter, nothing God created is intrinsically evil. But all things may be corrupted by sin. Sin is not material or tangible—it is a spiritual defect that infects all people. Whether we eat freely of everything or discipline ourselves by following certain dietary laws, what is our motivation?

2. How do those who understand the freedom of the Gospel respond to those who uphold certain dietary laws? Why?

3. On the other hand, if you are convinced certain foods or drinks should be avoided, how do you respond to those who insist on their freedom under the Gospel?

4. Read Genesis 1:29–30. What did Adam and Eve eat before their fall into sin? Now read Genesis 9:1–3. What did God allow Noah and his descendants to eat? What does this suggest about the repercussions of sin in the world?

> Then God said, "I give you every seed-bearing plant on the face of the whole earth and every tree that has fruit with seed in it. They will be yours for food. And to all the beasts of the earth and all the birds of the air and all the creatures that move on the ground—everything that has the breath of life in it—I give every green plant for food." And it was so. Genesis 1:29–30

> Then God blessed Noah and his sons, saying to them, "Be fruitful and increase in number and fill the earth. The fear and dread of you will fall upon all the beasts of the earth and all the birds of the air, upon every creature that moves along the ground, and upon all the fish of the sea; they are given into your hands. Everything that lives and moves will be food for you. Just as I gave you the green plants, I now give you everything." Genesis 9:1–3

5. The apostle Peter was born and raised a Jew, so the liberty of the Gospel was difficult for him to accept at first. Read Galatians 2:11–16. How did Peter demonstrate his weak faith when in the company of Jewish Christians? Who rebuked him and how did he do it? The Lord revealed a truth about clean and unclean foods to Peter in Acts 10:9–16. Describe the incident.

When Peter came to Antioch, I opposed him to his face, because he was clearly in the wrong. Before certain men came from James, he used to eat with the Gentiles. But when they arrived, he began to draw back and separate himself from the Gentiles because he was afraid of those who belonged to the circumcision group. The other Jews joined him in his hypocrisy, so that by their hypocrisy even Barnabus was led astray.

When I saw that they were not acting in line with the truth of the gospel, I said to Peter in front of them all, "You are a Jew, yet you live like a Gentile and not like a Jew. How is it, then, that you force Gentiles to follow Jewish customs?

"We who are Jews by birth and not 'Gentile sinners' know that a man is not justified by observing the law, but by faith in Jesus Christ. So we, too, have put our faith in Christ Jesus that we may be justified by faith in Christ and not by observing the law, because by observing the law no one will be justified." Galatians 2:11–16

About noon the following day as they were on their journey and approaching the city, Peter went up on the roof to pray. He became hungry and wanted something to eat, and while the meal was being prepared, he fell into a trance. He saw heaven opened and something like a large sheet being let down to earth by its four corners. It contained all kinds of four-footed animals, as well as reptiles of the earth and birds of the air. Then a voice told him, "Get up, Peter. Kill and eat."

"Surely not, Lord!" Peter replied. "I have never eaten anything impure or unclean."

The voice spoke to him a second time, "Do not call anything impure that God has made clean."

This happened three times, and immediately the sheet was taken back to heaven. Acts 10:9–16

6. For many Jewish Christians, it was a culture shock to witness hordes of Gentiles coming to faith in the Lord Jesus. The Gentiles had no problem accepting their freedom and liberty under the Gospel. For the Jews, the transition was not easy. The earliest council of Christian leaders hotly debated the issue of whether Gentile Christians should be forced to obey many Jewish laws. This council was held in Jerusalem and was attended by such great church leaders as Peter, Paul, Barnabas, and James. Look up Acts 15:1–19. What was the outcome of the Jerusalem Council? What conclusions did the council reach about the Gentiles?

The True Source of Evil (Romans 14:9–18)

1. Focus on Romans 14:17. Does righteousness and unrighteousness come from outward actions and rituals? Or do they arise from inside the individual's heart and spirit? What does Jesus have to say about this in Mark 7:14–23?

> Again Jesus called the crowd to Him and said, "Listen to Me, everyone, and understand this. Nothing outside a man can make him 'unclean' by going into him. Rather, it is what comes out of a man that makes him 'unclean.'"
>
> After He had left the crowd and entered the house, His disciples asked Him about this parable. "Are you so dull?" He asked. "Don't you see that nothing that enters a man from the outside can make him 'unclean'? For it doesn't go into his heart but into his stomach, and then out of his body." (In saying this, Jesus declared all foods "clean.")
>
> He went on: "What comes out of a man is what makes him 'unclean.' For from within, out of men's hearts, come evil thoughts, sexual immorality, theft, murder, adultery, greed, malice, deceit, lewdness, envy, slander, arrogance and folly. All these evils come from inside and make a man 'unclean.'" Mark 7:14–23

2. The Bible says we must all stand before the judgment seat of God (Romans 14:10; 2 Corinthians 5:10). This could be a fearful thought! Even though all of us must be judged, how does God judge believers in Christ (John 3:18)? How does God judge unbelievers? (John 3:18)

Whoever believes in Him is not condemned, but whoever does not believe stands condemned already because he has not believed in the name of God's one and only Son. John 3:18

Living in Peace and Unity (Romans 14:19–23)

1. Whether one eats meat or is a vegetarian, what principle controls our behavior toward those who disagree, according to Romans 14:19?

2. Paul concludes this chapter with an interesting comment. According to Romans 14:23, if someone does something she or he believes is wrong, is it a sin even if it does not violate God's Law? Why or why not? How might this understanding help us be more patient with those who insist that *adiaphora* (matters neither commanded nor forbidden by Scripture) are requirements of God's Law?

Applying the Message

1. Consider the possibility that God has made nothing intrinsically evil. Give examples of how people use for evil purposes what God has given. How is evil created—from the object or material, or from the hearts of those who use things for destructive purposes?

2. Alcohol is a good example of a drink that can be used for good or evil. How is it used for good, according to Matthew 26:26–29 and 1 Timothy 5:23? But in what way is it used for evil (Ephesians 5:18)? If a Christian views alcohol as something evil, what should be our attitude toward her or him? Should the Christian flaunt his or her right to drink? Why or why not?

> While they were eating, Jesus took bread, gave thanks and broke it, and gave it to His disciples, saying, "Take and eat; this is My body."
>
> Then He took the cup, gave thanks and offered it to them, saying, "Drink from it, all of you. This is My blood of the covenant, which is poured out for many for the forgiveness of sins. I tell you, I will not drink of this fruit of the vine from now on until that day when I drink it anew with you in My Father's kingdom." Matthew 26:26–29

> Stop drinking only water, and use a little wine because of your stomach and your frequent illnesses. 1 Timothy 5:23

> Do not get drunk on wine, which leads to debauchery. Instead, be filled with the Spirit. Ephesians 5:18

3. Can you think of any churches that have insisted on dietary restrictions? What are their restrictions? After reading Romans 14, explain how you would respond to those who preach certain foods are evil and should be avoided.

4. Is every substance created by God appropriate to consume? This could give pause for reflection. For example, how about cigarettes? Should the Christian view smoking as *adiaphora* neither commanded nor forbidden by Scripture? Of course, there is no specific prohibition against smoking in Scripture, but what about 1 Corinthians 6:19–20? When we know a certain substance harms our God-given bodies, is our consumption *adiaphora*?

> Do you not know that your body is a temple of the Holy Spirit, who is in you, whom you have received from God? You are not your own; you were bought at a price. Therefore honor God with your body. 1 Corinthians 6:19–20

Taking the Message Home

Review

When reviewing Romans 14, try to apply Paul's words to certain behaviors. Under what circumstances is it right or wrong for Christians to dance? To celebrate Halloween? To gamble? To read literature with certain risqué scenes?

Looking Ahead

As time permits, read Romans 15 and 16. Scan the list of names in chapter 16, but focus more carefully on Romans 16:17–20. Reflect on the possible motives of those who seem determined to provoke conflict within the community of God's people.

Working Ahead

Complete one or more of the following suggestions before the next session:

1. Write down the names of those whom Paul greets in Romans 16. How many are women? How many members of the Roman church are already acquainted with Paul?

2. Make a conscious effort this week to pray for your pastor and other spiritual leaders in the church. Pray that God will bless them with wisdom and courage so that they may lead according to His will. Then let your pastor know you are praying for him.

3. Reflect on the friends you have made during your lifetime. Are you still in touch with all of them? Where have they gone? List their names and locations. To which ones would you like to send greetings? What would you like to say to them?

Did You Know . . .

In the Old Testament, the Lord created a distinction between animals that were fit for eating and those that were to be avoided as unclean. Deuteronomy 14:3–21 gives us a partial list of these two categories. Clean foods included oxen, sheep, goats, deer, gazelles, and antelope, while camels, rabbits, and rock badgers were to be avoided. Pigs were considered unclean, as were fish that carried no fins or scales. Many birds were considered clean, except for eagles, vultures, falcon, ravens, many owls, storks, herons, and bats (although today we would not classify a bat as a bird). Flying insects and any animals that were already dead were considered unclean. To the contemporary reader, there is no apparent pattern to these prohibitions. Some have wondered whether the Lord defined animals as clean or unclean depending on their health benefits, but this distinction is not upheld by close examination. More than anything, the division between clean and unclean animals reflected God's desire to create a separate and holy people. The children of Israel were to be different than other nations of the world; many of their dietary laws would emphasize their chosen status. They were to be viewed as unique ambassadors to the true God. To this day, orthodox Jews are proud of their dietary laws and eat foods that are kosher.

Session 12

Encouragement, Plans, and Greetings

(Romans 15–16)

Approaching This Study

Paul certainly has not been timid about expressing his beliefs to the Christians in Rome! Rather than suggest that the Jewish Christians and Gentile Christians separate and enjoy their homogenous congregations, Paul exhorts them to work together. They are to sacrifice a part of themselves for the purpose of building up one another and strengthening one another in the faith.

How radical his message is! Even today, most Christians ask themselves, "What can I get out of the church?" rather than, "What can I give to my community of believers?" Too many Christians criticize and insult those who annoy them rather than demonstrate patience and tolerance for their weaknesses. Believers recognize that the call of Christ requires temporal sacrifice. Sacrifice is an essential ingredient in spiritual growth. Our growing faith is demonstrated through our spiritual uplifting of others. Paul's exhortation for Christians to bear one another's burdens continues in this chapter. As he underscores his own mission to the Gentiles, he relates his plans to journey where no disciple has yet traveled. He intends to travel to the farthest reaches of the Roman Empire, even as far as Spain. But he will visit the church in Rome first. In preparation for that visit, he concludes his letter with greetings from a number of Christians in Corinth.

An Overview

Unit Reading

Read Romans 15. If time is short, read only verses 1–5 and 16–27 from chapter 16. No one should be too concerned about the accurate pronunciation of the names.

The Message in Brief

As Paul continues his discussion of the Christian's response to God's grace and election, he describes his ministry as one particularly focused on the Gentiles who have never before heard the Gospel message. He exhorts the Roman Christians to accept one another, despite their varying backgrounds, and to support one another in unity under the Lord Jesus Christ. Then Paul expresses his plans to visit the Roman Christians on his way to Spain. First, however, he must bring an offering collected by some of the Gentile Christian churches for the poorer Jewish Christians in Jerusalem. Finally, Paul sends his own personal greetings as well as greetings from those in Corinth who have friends in Rome, interspersing these greetings with some final warnings about those who are compelled to divide a church rather than uplift it. He concludes with a word of praise to God and His Son, Jesus.

Working with the Text

Encouraging One Another (Romans 15:1–13)

1. Paul reminds the Roman Christians that Jesus came as a servant to the Jews to confirm the Old Testament promises given to the founders of Judaism (Abraham, Isaac, Jacob, and Jacob's twelve sons). The first Christian martyr, Stephen, was put to death for preaching this theme in-depth before the Jewish religious authorities in Jerusalem. Read Acts 7:1–53 and summarize Stephen's sermon.

2. Where must Christians find their unity, according to Romans 15:4? Consider 2 Timothy 3:16–17. If we have religious differences of opinion with our Christian sisters and brothers, where must we first look to find resolution?

All Scripture is God-breathed and is useful for teaching, rebuking, correcting and training in righteousness, so that the man of God may be thoroughly equipped for every good work. 2 Timothy 3:16–17

3. In Romans 15:9–12, where does Paul find his support for evangelizing the Gentiles? The early church hotly debated the question of whether Gentiles could be considered "children of God." How does Paul use God's Word to resolve this difference of opinion?

Paul's Ministry to the Gentiles (Romans 15:14–22)

1. Paul believed he had been called to a specific task on behalf of God's church. What was that task, according to Romans 15:17–20?

2. Does Paul take the credit for his ministry? Whom does he credit for his successes (see Romans 15:18)? Was Paul consistent in giving God the glory? Read Acts 15:12 and 21:19.

> The whole assembly became silent as they listened to Barnabas and Paul telling about the miraculous signs and wonders God had done among the Gentiles through them. Acts 15:12

> Paul greeted them and reported in detail what God had done among the Gentiles through his ministry. Acts 21:19

3. Romans 15:14 describes Paul's confidence in the Roman Christians. How do they stand in their understanding of Christian doctrine and their ability to teach God's Word? Nonetheless, Paul has written

them boldly about some concerns. After reading this letter, how would you summarize Paul's major worries about the Roman church? No church or congregation is perfect. Each carries with it strengths and weaknesses. Looking at your own congregation, what do you think are its strengths? Its weaknesses? What gifts do you have that you could use to strengthen your congregation?

Paul's Upcoming Plans (Romans 15:23–33)

1. When does Paul hope to visit the Christians in Rome (Romans 15:24, 28)? What must he do first (Romans 15:25–27)? With what attitude did the Gentiles in Macedonia and Achaia raise their offerings? What does this suggest about the depth of their faith? What does this, along with 2 Corinthians 9:6–7, suggest about our attitude in offering part of our material blessings to the Lord?

> Remember this: Whoever sows sparingly will also reap sparingly, and whoever sows generously will also reap generously. Each man should give what he has decided in his heart to give, not reluctantly or under compulsion, for God loves a cheerful giver. 2 Corinthians 9:6–7

2. For what does Paul ask the Roman Christians to pray concerning his work (Romans 15:31–32)? Now read Acts 21:27–32. What, in fact, happened to Paul when he arrived in Jerusalem? Interestingly, this sad experience was used by God to bring Paul to Rome. After Paul was arrested, a number of Jews plotted to kill Paul. When a Roman commander learned about the plot, he transferred Paul to Caesarea to be judged by Felix, the governor. But Felix left Paul in custody for two years until Felix was replaced by Festus, who wanted to return Paul to Jerusalem for trial. Paul, being a Roman citizen, had the right to appeal to Caesar and did so. Festus acknowledged Paul's right, and transferred Paul to Rome. It may have taken much longer than he expected, but Paul finally accomplished his desire to meet the Christians in Rome!

When the seven days were nearly over, some Jews from the province of Asia saw Paul at the temple. They stirred up the whole crowd and seized him, shouting, "Men of Israel, help us! This is the man who teaches all men everywhere against our people and our law and this place. And besides, he has brought Greeks into the temple area and defiled this holy place." (They had previously seen Trophimus the Ephesian in the city with Paul and assumed that Paul had brought him into the temple area.)

The whole city was aroused, and the people came running from all directions. Seizing Paul, they dragged him from the temple, and immediately the gates were shut. While they were trying to kill him, news reached the commander of the Roman troops that the whole city of Jerusalem was in an uproar. He at once took some officers and soldiers and ran down to the crowd. When the rioters saw the commander and his soldiers, they stopped beating Paul. Acts 21:27–32

Final Greetings (Romans 16)

1. As Paul concluded his letter, he sent greetings from himself and from Christians in and around Corinth. One of the individuals he mentioned was a woman named Phoebe who served the church in Cenchrea. Cenchrea was a port village resting only about six miles east of Corinth. What does Paul say about Phoebe?

2. Two other Christians were named Priscilla and Aquila. Where did the church in Corinth meet according to Romans 16:5? Now read Acts 18:1–2. Where did Paul first meet Priscilla and Aquila? Why were they in Corinth? From where did they originally come?

After this, Paul left Athens and went to Corinth. There he met a Jew named Aquila, a native of Pontus, who had recently come from Italy with his wife Priscilla, because Claudius had ordered all the Jews to leave Rome. Acts 18:1–2

3. According to Paul, why are some people motivated to cause divisions in the church, placing obstacles in the way of people's faith (Romans 16:17–18)?

4. In Romans 16:23, Paul sends greetings from a man named Gaius. According to 1 Corinthians 1:14, how was Gaius brought to the Lord ? Gaius and Crispus are mentioned together in 1 Corinthians 1:14. Acts 18:7–8 links them to Paul's ministry in Corinth. Many people believe Titius Justus is Gaius, his full name being Gaius Titius Justus!

I am thankful that I did not baptize any of you except Crispus and Gaius. 1 Corinthians 1:14

Then Paul left the synagogue and went next door to the house of Titius Justus, a worshiper of God. Crispus, the synagogue ruler, and his entire household believed in the Lord; and many of the Corinthians who heard him believed and were baptized. Acts 18:7–8

Applying the Message

1. Paul understood his ministry as one that would focus on reaching the Gentiles in areas never before evangelized. The call of a pastor and the mission of his church depend a great deal on the location and culture of the congregation. If you were to describe your congregation's ministry, what would it be?

2. One of the radical aspects of Christianity is its call to sacrifice for the sake of others. This call remains unpopular among most people today. Why does sacrificing for others ultimately bring us more fulfillment and joy than constantly focusing on our own needs and concerns?

3. For Christians a tension exists between the desire for Christian unity and the need for sound doctrine. In Romans 15:5–6, Paul calls on us to pursue unity with one another so that we may glorify God with one voice. Look at Jude 3–4 and notice the importance of remaining separate from those who pervert the Gospel of Jesus Christ. When do you think it is appropriate to accept the differences others have from our beliefs about Jesus? When must you view their ideas as unacceptable?

> Dear friends, although I was very eager to write to you about the salvation we share, I felt I had to write and urge you to contend for the faith that was once for all entrusted to the saints. For certain men whose condemnation was written about long ago have secretly slipped in among you. They are godless men, who change the grace of our God into a license for immorality and deny Jesus Christ our only Sovereign and Lord. Jude 3–4

4. Paul urges the Christians in Rome to accept each other. And he encourages those who are strong in their faith to bear the failings of those who are weaker in the faith. Consider your own congregation. What blessings do you think are given to those Christians who accept and love their brothers and sisters in the church, even though some individuals may be difficult to love or spiritually immature?

Taking the Message Home

Review

Read over the last verses of Paul's letter (Romans 16:25–27). Consider the reason Paul gives for the Bible's existence. What is the ultimate purpose of God's Word? Look up John 20:31 and notice how John describes the purpose of his narration. If the Word of God is important for salvation, what plans do you have to remain faithful in Bible study?

Looking Ahead

List the important understandings you gained from your study of Romans. How has Paul's letter affected your perspective about the Lord and His church? How has it influenced your understanding of God's grace and election? What practical impact do you think this will have in your life?

Working Ahead

In Paul's day, Christians would often greet one another with a "holy kiss" (Romans 16:16). Today, people are more comfortable greeting one another with a handshake. Before closing this session, each person in the group should turn to her or his neighbor, shake that individual's hand and say, "You have been chosen by God to live with Him forever. To the only wise God be glory forever through Jesus Christ. Amen." How might participants continue to have opportunities to greet one another? How might these opportunities help to build each other up in the faith?

Did You Know . . .

Near the end of this letter, Paul sends greetings to the Roman church from "Erastus, who is the city's director of public works." (Romans 16:23) While digging around in the ruins of Corinth, archaeologists uncovered a block of stone in a paved square. On this stone was engraved in Latin, "Erastus, commissioner of public works, bore the expense of this pavement." It seems likely this is the same individual for whom Paul sends greetings. It also supports the belief held by many scholars that Paul wrote this letter while staying in Corinth on his third missionary journey, around A.D. 57.

From *The Doré Bible Illustrations*. By permission of Dover Publications, Inc.

Glossary

adultery. Consensual sexual intercourse between a person and another person's spouse. Jesus interprets the Sixth Commandment, which forbids adultery, as forbidding all kinds of sexual indecency in both deed and thought (Matthew 5:28).

amen. The word *amen* is spoken when one wants to express "so be it." It indicates confirmation or agreement.

angels. Literally "messengers." Most often used to refer to spiritual, heavenly beings who were created by God. Some angels, led by Satan, rebelled against God. Holy angels, who did not rebel, continually do God's bidding. They protect and serve people who have faith in God. Angels differ in rank.

anoint. To apply oil to a person or thing. Sometimes anointing was simply a part of grooming. After washing or bathing, people anointed themselves. Hosts anointed their guests as an act of courtesy or respect. Anointing was also done at a person's induction into the office of priest, king, or sometimes prophet to indicate that the person was being set apart for that particular service. Christ was anointed with the Holy Spirit.

Antichrist. One who is both an enemy of Christ and a usurper of His rights and names.

apocalyptic literature. A type of literature that is highly symbolic and deals with the revelation of mysteries, especially concerning the end times. Biblical examples of this type of literature include Daniel 7–12 and Revelation. Apocalyptic literature, usually written in times of oppression, was primarily meant to encourage God's people.

apostles. Used several times in a general sense to mean "messengers," in the New Testament this word most often refers to those who were specifically commissioned by Jesus to proclaim the Gospel. Most prominent of the apostles were the Twelve and Paul. The teaching of the apostles, along with that of the prophets, is the foundation of the church. *See also* disciples.

Baptism. Christian Baptism—the application of water in the name of the triune God (Father, Son, and Holy Spirit) is a sacrament. The way the water is applied to the individual can vary. The New Testament makes no distinction between adult and infant Baptism. Christian Baptism works the forgiveness of sins; it delivers one from spiritual death and the devil; it gives eternal salvation to all who believe in Christ; it confers the Holy Spirit. Baptism also makes one a member of the body of Christ, the church. *See also* sacrament.

Bethlehem. The birthplace of Jesus Christ, thus fulfilling the Old Testament prophecy found in Micah 5:2.

Capernaum. The center of Jesus' Galilean ministry. The site of some of His early miracles and of the calling of some of His disciples.

Christ. Greek for the Hebrew word *Messiah,* which means "Anointed One." Throughout the Old Testament God promised to send the Messiah to deliver His people from their enemies and to set up His kingdom. Jesus is that Messiah.

church. The collective gathering of God's people. The New Testament speaks of the church both as the Christians gathered in a specific place and as all Christians everywhere of all time. It is also described as the fellowship of God's people, the bride of Christ, the body of Christ, and a building of which Jesus Christ is the chief cornerstone.

circumcision. Removal of the foreskin of the penis. Circumcision was a stipulation of the covenant God made with Abraham and his descendants. It showed that He would be their God, and they were to belong to Him. Controversy erupted in the early Christian church about whether Gentile Christians needed to be circumcised. St. Paul spoke God's Word to this controversy when he declared that circumcision was not required of Gentiles who became Christians.

congregation. An assembly of people gathered for worship and religious instruction; a collective, religious group.

conversion. An act of God's grace by which a sinful person is turned around and brought into God's kingdom. Conversion is accomplished by the Holy Spirit, who brings the person to faith in Christ through the Word.

covenant. An agreement between two or more tribes, nations, or individuals in which one or all of the parties promise under oath to do or refrain from doing something. Scripture records a number of covenants God has made with His people.

deacon. Someone who serves. In the early church, deacons were chosen to relieve the apostles of caring for the physical needs of widows and other poor people.

demons. Evil spirits who are against God and His work. They are angels who rebelled against God and now follow Satan.

disciples. Students or learners. In the New Testament disciples most often refers to Jesus' followers. Sometimes it refers specifically to the Twelve, but often it applies to a larger group of those who followed Jesus and learned from His teaching. *See also* apostles.

doctrine. Instruction or teaching; a body of beliefs about such theological issues as God, Christ, humanity, the church, and salvation.

Easter. Originally a pagan festival honoring a Teutonic (ancient Germanic) goddess of light and spring. By the eighth century the name was applied to the commemoration of Christ's resurrection.

elder. In the New Testament, *elder* and *bishop* are both used to mean "oversees." The elder or presbyter was a man the apostles appointed in each Christian congregation to be its spiritual leader.

elect. The elect are those who have faith in Christ as the promised Messiah and Savior.

election. The doctrine that explains the biblical truth that God from eternity planned our salvation and chose by His grace those who will be saved in Christ. No one deserves to be saved. God, however, desires that all people be saved. By God's grace through faith alone in Jesus, people (the elect) are saved. Those who have received God's gift of faith respond in thankfulness to God for His love and grace in choosing them.

epistle. A formal letter; one of the letters adopted as books of the New Testament.

eternal life. Abiding fellowship with God of infinite duration. Eternal life begins when the Holy Spirit by grace brings a person to faith in Jesus Christ. Although the Christian already has eternal life, he or she will not experience it fully until the resurrection of the dead and the life of the world to come.

faith. The belief and trust in the promise of God in Christ Jesus, worked by the Holy Spirit, through which a person is brought into a right relationship with God and saved. The Holy Spirit works faith in Christ in the individual through Word and Sacrament.

fellowship. Sharing something in common. By grace, through faith in Christ, God has given believers fellowship, that is, an intimate relationship, with Himself. Through the work of the Holy Spirit, fellow believers also have a oneness in Christ and share with one another the common bond of the Gospel and faith in Christ.

forgiveness. God's act whereby He ends the separation caused by peoples' sins and restores people to a proper relationship with Him. Forgiveness is a gift of God, given out of grace for Christ's sake. As a result of Christ's forgiveness, we are to forgive our neighbor. Recognizing that we are sinful and being sorry for our sins precedes forgiveness.

Gentiles. Non-Hebrew peoples of the world; people outside the Jewish faith.

glory. That which shows the greatness of someone or something. The glory of God is shown in and by His great miracles, His eternal perfection, His creation, and all His works. Most important, it is shown by His Son, our Lord Jesus Christ, and the salvation He won for all people.

Gnosticism. A belief system that reached its peak in the second and third centuries A.D. According to the Gnostics, salvation came by hating the world and everything physical and by escaping to the spirit world through special knowledge. Gnostics said Jesus came not to save people from sin but to show them how to escape to the spiritual world.

Gospel (Good News). The message that Jesus Christ has fulfilled the Law for all people and paid the penalty for their sin on the cross, thus having won forgiveness and salvation for them.

gospels. The first four books of the New Testament. Matthew, Mark, Luke, and John each wrote one of the books. They are called gospels because they tell the good news of how salvation was won for all people by Jesus Christ.

grace. God's undeserved love and favor revealed in Jesus Christ by which He is moved to forgive people's sins and grant them salvation. The word *grace* is sometimes used to mean a gift, quality, or virtue. Saving grace, however, is none of these things. It is a quality within God. It is also referred to as God's steadfast love or faithfulness.

heaven. The invisible world or universe from which God rules; the home of angels. Christ rules from heaven and receives believers there. *See also* paradise.

heir. The individual to whom another person's wealth or possessions—the person's inheritance—is given after the person dies.

hell. The place of eternal punishment or the punishment itself.

112

heresy. Stubborn error in an article of faith in opposition to Scripture.

holy. Without sin; an essential aspect of God's nature. Those who trust in Christ for salvation have been declared holy and righteous in God's sight. The Holy Spirit, through the Gospel, works in believers to motivate and empower them to lead lives of holiness. *Holy* can also be used to refer to something set apart to be used for or by God.

hymn. A song telling about God and praising Him.

inspiration. The special way the Holy Spirit worked in certain people to cause them to act out, speak, or write God's Word. When the Holy Spirit did this, the person who was inspired was certainly under the direction of God's power, but he or she was not a robot. As Paul says, "All Scripture is God-breathed" (2 Timothy 3:16).

Israel. (1) The name given to Jacob after he wrestled with God (Genesis 32:28). (2) The name of the nation composed of the descendants of Jacob and his 12 sons. Jacob and his sons founded the 12 tribes of Israel. (3) The name given to the 10 northern tribes of Israel after Solomon's death, when they revolted against Rehoboam and the kingdom split in two. The Northern Kingdom was called Israel to distinguish it from the Southern Kingdom, which was called Judah. (4) All who follow in the faith of Abraham, Isaac, and Jacob and therefore are true Israelites, no matter what their physical descent.

Jerusalem. The state and religious capital of the Hebrew nation. Jesus was arrested, tried, and crucified in Jerusalem.

Jesus. Greek for the Hebrew name *Joshua,* which means "Yahweh (the LORD) saves."

Jew. A later derivation of the word *Judean,* which referred to someone who belonged to the tribe or kingdom of Judah (Southern Kingdom) as opposed to the Northern Kingdom. *Hebrew* denotes those who descended from Abraham through Isaac and Jacob; *Israel* denotes those who descended from Jacob; and *Judean,* later *Jew,* denotes those who descended from the tribe or kingdom of Judah. As well as being an ethnic designation, the term *Jew* also refers to the adherents of a religion. While in New Testament times some Jews were faithful adherents of the faith of the Old Testament, others had begun to deviate from that faith. During the time between the Old and New Testaments, a number of Jewish religious groups had developed, such as the Pharisees and the Sadducees. The pharisaic branch survived after New Testament times and has most influenced the religion called Judaism, which is composed of a combination of oral tradition and Old Testament beliefs. *See also* Pharisees.

Jordan River. The river that connects the Sea of Galilee to the Dead Sea. It is the river in which Jesus was baptized by John.

Judah. (1) The fourth son of Jacob and Leah. Jacob bestowed the blessing of the birthright on Judah. Jesus was one of Judah's descendants. (2) The tribe that descended from Judah. It occupied the greater part of southern Palestine. (3) The kingdom of Judah, which began when the 10 northern tribes withdrew from Rehoboam around 930 B.C. The kingdom of Judah, which occupied the southern part of Palestine, lasted until 586 B.C., when Jerusalem fell to the Babylonians.

justification. The gracious act of God by which He pronounces people to be not guilty of their sin through faith in Jesus. The basis for His acquittal is that Jesus Christ fulfilled the Law in humanity's place and paid the penalty for all people's sin by His suffering and death on the cross.

kingdom of God. A spiritual kingdom, ruled by God, that includes people from all nations. The New Testament sometimes pictures God's kingdom as the rule of the Holy Spirit in the hearts of God's people. The kingdom of God is, at times, spoken of as a future blessing, as in the kingdom Jesus will bring on the Last Day, and, at times, described as a present reality. The church proclaims the kingdom of God by preaching the Gospel.

Lord. (1) LORD (printed in capital and small capital letters) is the way *Yahweh*, God's personal name in the Old Testament, is often rendered in English. (2) Lord (capital *L* and the remaining letters lowercase) comes from the Hebrew word *adon*. It means "master" and denotes ownership. (3) At some point, probably after the exile, God's people stopped pronouncing *Yahweh* and instead said *Adonai* whenever they saw the consonants for *Yahweh* (YHWH) in the Hebrew Bible. (4) The Greek word *kyrios* is also translated as Lord. It is the word used for a human master or for God as ruler, and is also used to refer to Christ.

Lord's Supper. Christ instituted this supper on the night of His betrayal. It is to be celebrated in the church until His return as a proclamation of His death for the sins of the world. In this meal, Christ gives His body and blood in, with, and under the bread and wine. Christians who trust in the blessings Christ promises to give in this meal and who partake of it in faith receive through it forgiveness of sins, life, salvation, and a strengthening of their faith. Also called "Breaking of Bread," "Holy Communion," "Eucharist," and "the Lord's Table."

love. Various types of love are referred to in the Bible. The Greek word *agape* represents God's sacrificial and intentional love for sinful people. This is the kind of love Christians are to have.

mercy. The aspect of God's character that moves Him to spare us from hurtful things even though we deserve them and to help those in distress. As Christians have been shown mercy by God, they are to be merciful to others.

Messiah. Hebrew for "Anointed One." *See also* Christ.

minister. A person who has been called—by God, through the church—to spiritually feed and care for God's people. All Christians have vocations—callings by God in life. All Christians have received various gifts of the Holy Spirit for the building up of others in the church. All Christians are members of the priesthood of all believers (1 Peter 2:9). However, just as Jesus chose 12 of His disciples to serve as apostles, God distinctly calls some people to be ministers.

miracle. An event that causes wonder; something that takes place outside of the laws of nature. The New Testament depicts miracles as signs, wonders, and acts of power. Their significance could be understood only by those who had faith in Jesus Christ.

Nazareth. Jesus' hometown. The place where He grew up after His family returned from Egypt. Jesus was not well received in Nazareth when He returned during His ministry.

ordination. A rite (act) of the church by which the church through a congregation publicly confers the pastoral office on a qualified man. Ordination has its historical roots in the New Testament and in the early church. In the New Testament, deacons, missionaries, and elders were called to their offices, just as today a congregation calls a man to be its pastor.

parable. An earthly story with a heavenly or spiritual meaning: a saying or story that uses an illustration from everyday life for the purpose of teaching a moral or religious truth. Although the events and characters in the parable are true to nature, not every detail of the story has a spiritual meaning. Rather, there is only one main point of comparison. Jesus often spoke in parables to teach the people about Himself and the kingdom of heaven.

paradise. Used in the New Testament to describe heaven, the home of those who die in Christ. *See also* heaven.

peace. Often used to describe that state of spiritual tranquility and harmony that God gives when He brings one into a right relationship with Himself.

Pentecost. The Jewish Feast of Weeks, which was celebrated 50 days after the offering of the barley sheaf during the Feast of Unleavened Bread. Pentecost is also known as the Feast of Harvest and the Day of Firstfruits. On this day the Holy Spirit was poured out on the disciples, and many people came to faith in Christ after hearing Peter's Spirit-filled preaching.

Pharisees. One of several Jewish religious parties in New Testament times, primarily made up of people from the middle class. They were characterized by scrupulous keeping of the mosaic law and the oral traditions added to the Law. It was their desire to make the Law understandable and applicable so that people might fully obey it. Thus, they formulated lists of rules, spelling out exactly, for example, what constituted work on the Sabbath. In this way they sought to build a "fence" around the Law to keep people from getting close to violating its commandments. In general, the Jews highly respected the Pharisees. Some Pharisees, such as Nicodemus, were sincere in their beliefs, but many others fell into hypocrisy, living by the letter of the Law and not following its spirit.

prayer. Speaking with God. Prayers can be formal or spoken freely from one's own thoughts and concerns. They can be said together by a group of believers or alone by an individual. They can be said at set times and in set places or at all times and in all places.

priests. One who represents the people before God. Through Moses, God appointed Aaron and his descendants as priests. They wore special clothing in the sanctuary, taught the people, and inquired of God's will. The chief priest, or high priest, was in charge of all other priests. He offered the sin offering, made sacrifice on the Day of Atonement, and discovered the will of God through Urim and Thummim. In the New Testament, Jesus Christ is the only high priest. Since He sacrificed Himself for the sins of the people and this sacrifice need never be repeated, there is no longer a need for the Levitical priesthood. The New Testament also teaches the priesthood of all believers. Christians share in Christ's priestly activity by bringing the Gospel to people.

Redeemer. The one who buys back. Jesus Christ. *See also* redemption.

redemption. The buying back of humanity from sin and death by Christ, the Redeemer, who paid the price with His perfect obedience and His sacrificial death on the cross.

repentance. A total change of heart and life that God works in an individual who does not believe or trust in Him by turning him or her around to believe and trust in Him. Repentance includes both sorrow for one's sins and faith in Christ through whom forgiveness is granted.

resurrection. A return to life after one has died.

righteous. That which is right in accordance with the Law. The term is particularly used to describe people who are in a right relationship with God through faith in Christ.

sacrament. A sacred act instituted by God where there are visible means connected to His Word. In a sacrament God offers, gives, and seals to the individual the forgiveness of sins earned by Christ.

sacrifice. An act of worship where a person presents an offering to God. God commanded sacrifices in the Old Testament as a way for sins to be atoned for and as a means for people to express thankfulness to Him. Among the main sacrifices mentioned in the Old Testament are the sin offering, the trespass offering, the burnt offering, the peace offering, and the meal and drink offerings. Among other times, offerings were sacrificed on the altar in the morning and evening, at each Sabbath and new moon, and at the three leading festivals. All sacrifices pointed to and were fulfilled in Christ, the Lamb of God, who was sacrificed for the sins of the world.

salvation. Deliverance from any type of evil, both physical and spiritual. Spiritual salvation includes rescue from sin. It is a gift of God's grace through faith in Christ.

Samaria. During Old Testament times, the capital city of the Northern Kingdom of Israel. During New Testament times, the land of the Samaritans between Galilee in the north and Judea in the south. Interestingly, the most direct route from Nazareth to Jerusalem led directly through Samaria; however, most Jews would avoid that route, taking a significant detour across the Jordan River and then south.

Samaritans. A mixed race of people descended partly from the tribes of the Northern Kingdom of Israel and partly from Gentiles settled in Israel during the exilic period of the Old Testament. The Samaritans worshiped the God of Israel, but their religion differed from that of the Jews in significant ways. For example, Samaritans accepted the authority of the Pentateuch only and rejected the rest of the Hebrew scriptures. Jews and Samaritans, although culturally very similar, lived on "opposite sides of the tracks." They were often bigoted toward each other and avoided each other. Jews thought that the Samaritans, like tax collectors, had no place in the messianic kingdom.

Satan. The chief fallen angel and enemy of God, humanity, and all that is good. Sometimes called Abaddon, Apollyon, or Beelzebul (Beelzebub).

Sea of Galilee. A body of water fed by the Jordan River. Jesus spent much of His early ministry around the Sea of Galilee. The sea is the place where Jesus walked on water and calmed the storm. During New Testament times, the sea (more properly considered a lake) supported a large fishing industry.

sin. Both doing what God forbids and failing to do what He commands. Because of sin everyone deserves temporal and eternal death. Only through faith in Christ, who kept God's Law perfectly and suffered the punishment for the sins of the world, does one escape the results of sin.

Son of God. A title applied to Jesus in a unique sense. It says that Jesus as the Son is equal to God the Father.

Son of Man. The term Jesus most often used to refer to Himself. This title emphasizes the power and dominion Jesus receives from the Ancient of Days. (See Daniel 7:9, 13–14 and Matthew 16:27.)

soul, spirit. The immaterial essence that animates the flesh. The soul (often called the spirit) is not separate from the body; rather it is that which gives life. It is the inner person as distinguished from the flesh. It is the seat of the appetites, emotions, and passions. The soul departs at death. It can be lost and saved.

Suffering Servant. A synonym for Jesus. Jesus is the fulfillment of the Suffering Servant prophesied in the Old Testament (Isaiah 42:1–4; 49:1–6; 50:4–9; 52:13–53:12).

tabernacle. The movable tent that God commanded His people to build after He delivered them from bondage in Egypt. God promised to dwell among His people in the tabernacle (Exodus 25:8). The tabernacle served as Israel's center of worship until Solomon's temple was built. *See also* temple.

tax collectors. In New Testament times, the people who collected taxes for the Roman Empire. Roman taxes were very high, and it was the practice of the empire to hand over the collection of taxes to individuals or businesses, who would add a certain percentage to the amount collected. Needless to say, this system, called "tax farming," was open to abuse. Most Jews hated tax collectors, viewing them as usurers and thieves who supported the godless Roman oppressors. Tax collectors were deemed unclean. They were cut off from the people of God and were thought to have no place in the messianic kingdom.

teachers of the law. Specialists in and teachers of Jewish ceremonial, civil, and moral laws.

temple. The fixed sanctuary of the Lord that replaced the tabernacle as God's dwelling place among His people. The temple was the center of Israelite and then Jewish worship until it was destroyed. Jesus, God who took on human flesh, replaced the temple as God's dwelling place among His people (John 1:14; John 2:19–21; Revelation 21:22). *See also* tabernacle.

testament. A document outlining the distribution of a person's property after death. When the Old Testament (originally written in Hebrew and Aramaic) was translated into Greek, the Hebrew word for "covenant" was translated with the Greek word for "testament." This same Greek word is used in Jesus' Words of Institution (see Mark 14:24) and is translated by some as "covenant" and by others as "testament." *See also* covenant.

tithe. A tenth part of one's income given as an offering to the Lord. According to the Law, a tenth of all produce of land and herds was sacred to the Lord.

transfiguration. The name given to the occasion when Jesus was visibly glorified in the presence of three of His disciples.

Trinity. The church's term for the coexistence of Father, Son, and Holy Spirit in the unity of the Godhead—three distinct persons in one divine being, or essence. The term *Trinity* does not occur in the Bible, but many passages support the doctrine of the Trinity.

unleavened bread. Bread made without yeast. The Israelites ate unleavened bread at Passover and the subsequent Feast of Unleavened Bread as a reminder of the haste with which they left Egypt during the exodus. During the exodus, they did not have time to bake bread but took with them unleavened dough that they baked in the wilderness.

will. Inclination or choice. God's will is revealed in His acts, His Law, and especially in Christ. Although the will of fallen human beings has some capacity to perform works that conform outwardly to God's Law, humanity's fallen or natural will cannot incline itself toward God or choose to have true faith in Him. Only the Holy Spirit working through the Gospel can create in people true faith in God, thereby inclining a person's will to good. *See also* works.

Word. God's Word is the means through which He makes Himself known and reveals His will to humanity. His Word is the primary way through which He works His purposes in the world. The Holy Scriptures are the written Word of God. They tell of the purpose of God in creating, saving, and sanctifying His people. They testify to Jesus Christ, the Word of God made flesh. Jesus Christ is the supreme revelation of God. He is the living Word.

works. Deeds. Whether a person's works are ultimately deemed good or bad in God's sight depends on that person's relationship to God. Only a person who believes in Jesus Christ as Savior can do good works in God's eyes, since good works are a fruit of faith.

world. Used in Scripture not only to describe the universe or the human race, but often to denote the wicked and the unbelieving, that is, those who are opposed to God.

worship. To bow down, kiss the hand, revere, or serve. The respect and reverence given to God. New Testament worship is centered in and around the Word of God. It involves reading Scripture, singing hymns and spiritual songs, teaching, praying, and celebrating the Lord's Supper. In Christian worship, God bestows His gifts of forgiveness, life, and salvation upon us through His Word and Sacraments, and we respond in thankfulness and praise.

Zealots. Members of an ultra nationalistic first-century A.D. Jewish political group. They were similar to the Pharisees in their general beliefs, but where the Pharisees might be ready to die for their faith, the Zealots were ready to kill for it. They advocated the use of force against the Romans.